ROMAN FURNITURE

ROMAN FURNITURE

A.T. CROOM

The
History
Press

First published in 2007 by Tempus Publishing

Reprinted in 2010 by
The History Press
The Mill, Brimscombe Port,
Stroud, Gloucestershire, GL5 2QG
www.thehistorypress.co.uk

British Library Cataloguing in Publication Data.
A catalogue record for this book is available from the British Library.

ISBN 978 0 7524 4097 2

Typesetting and origination by Tempus Publishing Limited
Printed in Great Britain

Contents

List of figures

List of colour plates

List of tables

Acknowledgements

Much of the preliminary research for this book was carried out whilst given the pleasant task of arranging for replica items of Roman furniture to be made for the reconstructed Commanding Officer's house and Barrack at Arbeia Roman Fort in South Shields. The need to fill complete rooms raised interesting questions about how furniture was used in combination with other pieces, rather than just being considered as individual items in isolation, which has resulted in the second section of the book. Thanks are due to Tyne and Wear Museums, for permission to use many examples of their replica furniture as illustrations in this book. Thanks must also be extended to Nodge Nolan for discussions on aspects of furniture production and use, to Roger Oram for help and advice on some of the illustrations and to Katherine Croom for the index. William Griffiths kindly agreed to look over the text and made both useful suggestions and corrections; any remaining faults and mistakes are the responsibility of the author.

1
Introduction

According to Roman law, 'furniture' consisted of: 'any apparatus belonging to the head of the household consisting of articles intended for everyday use which do not fall into any other category, as, for instance, Stores, Silver, Clothing, Ornaments, or Apparatus of the land or the house' (*Edicts of Justinian*, 33.7; Watson 1985). In greater detail, these are identified as: 'tables, table legs, three-legged Delphic tables, benches, stools, beds (including those inlaid with silver), mattresses, coverlets, slippers, water jugs, basins, wash-basins, candelabra, lamps and bowls. Likewise, common bronze vessels, that is ones which are not specially attributed to one place. Moreover, bookcases and cupboards. But there are those who rightly hold that bookcases and cupboards, if they are intended to contain books, clothing or utensils, are not included in furniture, because these objects themselves ... do not go with the apparatus of furniture' (*ibid.*, 33.2).

That the jurists themselves argued over exactly what constituted 'furniture' did not disconcert them; for 'nor is it surprising that the designation has changed along with the customs of the state and the use of the objects; for they used to use earthenware, wooden, glass or at the most bronze furniture, whereas now they use furniture of ivory, tortoiseshell and silver, and even of gold and jewels. Therefore it is proper to consider the category to which things belong, whether to Furniture rather than to Silver or Clothing, rather than the material of which they are made' (*ibid.*, 33.7).

This study will take a more modern view and will exclude the bronze vessels and lamps in favour of the beds, tables, seats and storage items now considered to be 'furniture'. It is a study mainly of form and design, taking evidence from three categories; art, literary evidence, and surviving items. There will be little discussion of chronological development as the evidence for major changes is slight, and there will be no survey of the methods of manufacture, as Mols (1999) has made a detailed study of the structure of the surviving wooden examples from Herculaneum, and has discussed furniture manufacture in some detail. Instead, this study sets out to give an over-view of the range of furniture available in the Roman world, at all levels of society, and will conclude with a discussion of the use of the furniture room by room.

The quality and quantity of furniture in a Roman house depended considerably on the wealth of the family. The town house or country villa of a rich man would consist of a large number of rooms, many with specific purposes, such as dining-room, retiring-room overlooking a garden and study. Pliny's description of his Laurentine villa, for example, mentions at least 27 rooms. The number of rooms is large, as one way of demonstrating wealth was to have duplicate rooms or suites of rooms to provide variety for both owner and guests. These rooms could have specific items or combinations of furniture associated with them not usually found elsewhere, such as three couches in the dining-room (*triclinia*), but in the end the use of furniture came down to personal preference.

In smaller apartments or houses the range of furniture used depended on the space available. At Herculaneum, no examples of the three dining-couches survive, but *biclinia* (two dining-couches) that took up less space were used in smaller rooms. In the poorest houses, the couch used for dining during the day would be used as a bed for sleeping at night; in these houses or apartments the rooms, and furniture, had to be multi-functional. In modern houses the dining-room in particular is often combined with the kitchen or living-room, but dual-function furniture such as the sofa-bed is built so that two different designs are combined so that when used as a bed it looks very different to when it is used as a sofa, unlike the Roman couch/bed.

THE EVIDENCE

The evidence from art, literature and archaeology will often be discussed separately, due to the well-known problem of fixing Latin terms to objects. During the early excavations at Pompeii, for example, the complete metal fittings from decorated beds were found, consisting of metal legs, thin strips from the bed-frame and plates that decorated the end of the pillow rest. Not understanding that these were decorative elements fitted to a (decayed) wooden bed, the excavators assumed they were elements from a largely bronze item of furniture, and pieced them together into a large stool (*1*; compare *2*). They then found a Latin term for the seat they had created in the *bisellium* ('seat for two'), a rather uncommon term for a seat of honour (see *46*). This identification can still be found reproduced today without correction.

1 The bronze elements of a couch from Pompeii, reconstructed as a large stool identified as a *bisellium* (*after Stefanelli 1990*)

There is also the problem of considering how reliable artistic evidence, such as on tombstones, is at reflecting furniture use in a certain area or province. In Britain most of the dining tables on tombstones are shown with plain, bulbous legs even though a number of shale legs have been found in the province that incorporate animals in their design, as used elsewhere in the Empire. In Germany a specific design of a folding table is shown on a number of tombstones but is not seen elsewhere in the Empire. Does this reflect a genuinely local fashion of table use, or simply a fashion by the artists for depicting such tables in the tombstone scenes? Were they in fact used just as extensively elsewhere in the Empire, but simply not shown on tombstones?

ATTITUDES TO FURNITURE

Much modern furniture is designed for comfortable relaxation, although a study of furniture history shows that items such as cushioned armchairs and sofas have only developed over the past couple of hundred years, and became the main item of living-room furniture for people of all classes even more recently. In the past a much more functional view of furniture has often been taken. The Roman attitude is a mixture of the two approaches, as while there were comfortable couches for reclining on at meals there were no upholstered sofas for sitting on when entertaining guests, and the most common form of seating was a backless stool: comfortable chairs with supportive backs were considered to have a hint of decadence about them.

It must also be remembered that in many ways it was a society that functioned with a lot fewer material possessions than today, so that most people had far fewer items of furniture and personal belongings to clutter up a room. Although storage furniture (shelves, cupboards and chests) were very common in the Roman world, there were less items to store. Children, for example, would have had very few toys needing space. Clothing was hugely more expensive in relative terms than now, and only the rich would have had problems storing all their clothes. The poor would only have had a few items each, and most of those could well have been stored on their beds to act as extra blankets. Others would have kept all their clothes in a single chest, without the need for the large wardrobes and chest of drawers considered unavoidable nowadays in an age when clothes are changed daily.

The rich, then as now, sometimes bought antique furniture at huge prices. However, instead of impressing guests with furniture made by master craftsmen, the Roman rich used the material the furniture was made from as the indicator of their wealth. The design of the bed or the table was of less importance than the use of silver, ivory or citrus-wood in its construction.

2

The materials used in furniture

FASHIONS

Although there is evidence of the adoption of Greek fashions in couches and dining-tables, there must have been many other changes in fashions in furniture design that can no longer be distinguished. Fenestella, who died in AD 21, recalled tortoiseshell trays coming into fashion at about 80 BC and that when he was a child they changed from small circular to square ones, while Varro recalls rectangular tables with one leg that were placed near the water tanks in *atria* when he was a boy (*Natural Histories*, 33.51.144; *On the Latin Language*, 5.125). Literary evidence shows some differences were originally regional, with Pliny mentioning that one Carvilius Pollio was the first person to add silver to his dining couches, although 'not to cover them entirely or make them in the Delos style, but in the Punic style', while fir was suitable 'for any kind of inlaid work whether in the Greek or the Campanian or the Sicilian style' (*Natural Histories*, 33.51.144; 16.82). He also records that the Gauls were the first to have used linen mattress cases and stuffing as well as fleece stuffing (*ibid.*, 8.73.192; 19.2.13). Although these fashions may have started as regional differences, they could easily spread throughout the Empire. The three legged dining table, for example, originally from Greece, became common in every province.

I WOOD

Wood, as a generally cheap and easily available material, was not used for items of furniture intended to impress guests. The exception to this was citrus-wood, which became the short-hand cliché for extravagant furniture. The most expensive woods had elaborate grain patterns, so woods cut from burrs were much admired. Pliny records two different burr patterns in maple wood, '[one] veined in a twistier pattern, while the [other] is covered with simpler markings, and if it were large enough for tables to be made from it would undoubtedly be preferred to citrus wood' (*Natural Histories,* 16.26.66-9).

Literary evidence is useful for giving an idea of which types of wood were used for different types of furniture, but as usual can never give the whole picture. The number of times citrus-wood tables are mentioned in texts would suggest they were one of the most common types of furniture available instead of the most rare, but they are mentioned so often precisely because they are unusual. There was little need to mention the commonplace, every-day items of furniture, made in the type of woods to be found in every household. Silver fir is hardly mentioned in literature as a material for making furniture, with Pliny merely suggesting it was good for interior woodwork and doors (*Natural Histories,* 16.225), and yet the majority of the pieces of furniture from Herculaneum that have been identified are made of this wood, simply because it was a common tree in the region. Most furniture makers must have used whatever wood was available locally, as recorded by Juvenal: 'in those days tables were home-made from local timber; if the south-west wind happened to bring down an old walnut tree, that is how the wood was used' (*Satires,* 11.117-9).

Decorative woods

Citrus (Colour plates 1-2)

Although this has been identified as *callitris quadrivalvis* in the past, it is more likely that it is *teraclinis articulata* (also known as sandarac tree, thuja or thuya; Mols 1999, 77). Pliny provides extensive information about the wood in his *Natural Histories* (13.30) because of its fame as a luxury item. The three most prized grain patterns were called 'tiger wood' (wavy lines), 'panther' (twisted spiral patterns) and 'peacock' (eyes). Less favoured was 'parsley wood' (thick clusters of grain), and the least popular of all were the more uniform grains. The highest value was given to wood 'of the colour of mead', with paler coloured woods apparently being preferred to darker ones.

'Table mania' was seen as the male equivalent to women's extravagancies in buying flawless pearls, and Pliny mentions tables costing over one million *sesterces,* 'the price of a large estate' (*ibid.*, 13.29.92). The wood came from Mauritania in North Africa, where the King owned a table *c.*1.4m in diameter and *c.*8cm thick, made up of two pieces of wood seamlessly joined together. Nomius, a freedman of the Emperor Tiberius, had one that was *c.*1.2m across and a rather unbelievable 28cm thick, and made from a single piece of wood. Such tables, although described as circular, the usual shape of Roman dining-tables, were much too large for dining-tables (which were usually about 0.5m in diameter) and were closer in size to the marble versions of the three-legged tables which were decorative rather than functional. The whole table was not usually made from wood, but had a citrus top and ivory (or ivory-veneered) legs. While tables are the most frequently mentioned item of furniture made of this wood, other references to extreme extravagance also mention couches and cupboards (Mols 1999, 77).

Maple (Colour plates 3-4, 6)

Pliny describes this as being second only to citrus in popularity and therefore also very expensive, probably because maple burrs can produce equally dramatic patterns, with varieties such as 'peacock' and 'thick-veined' providing the exotic grains so favoured by the rich (*Natural Histories*, 16.66-8; 16.185). Cheaper versions, not made from burrs, were also made, such as a maple table that lacked any dramatic veining (Martial, *Epigrams,* 14.90). A surviving table leg has been found at Bergkamen-Oberaden, Germany, and it has also been found used for seats and a chest (Ovid, *Fasti,* 3.359; Mols 1999, fn 408; *ibid.*, cat. no. 41).

Other woods

These were woods chosen for the quality of the wood-grain, and could either be used solid or as a veneer (see below). Another expensive wood was turpentine-wood (terebinth), which Pliny talks of in similar terms as citrus and maple, while Propertius refers to a 'bridal-bed of citrus wood, or turpentine-wood from Oricos' (*Poems*, 3.7.49). As ebony had to be imported from India or Ethiopia, it was automatically another expensive wood for the rich. However, the lack of references to it by first-century authors suggests it was never as popular as citrus, probably because it lacked a dramatic grain, and a general preference for light-coloured woods is suggested by Pliny (*Natural Histories*, 13.30.97; 16.27.69-70). Although there is no evidence to support the theory, it is possible ebony became more popular in the later-Roman period, when black became more generally fashionable (for example, in black-slipped drinking vessels and in jet and 'black' glass jewellery), including, in Britain, black shale table legs. Walnut, another dark wood, is mentioned in the literary record as being used for dining-tables, and it had been chosen for a tabletop at Herculaneum because of its decorative appearance (Mols 1999, 79; *colour plate 5*).

Wood for every-day furniture

Beech (colour plate 8)

Pliny describes this as an easily worked but brittle and soft wood, although flexible as a veneer. He refers to it as being the only wood suitable for scroll-cases and book-boxes, many of which were cylindrical in shape (*Natural Histories*, 16.84.229). Beech-wood with less interesting grains were used for cheaper furniture, such as the beech table Martial unfavourably contrasts with a citrus and ivory table (*Epigrams*, 2.43), while Columella mentions a chest of beech (*On Farming,* 12.47.5), and a turned beech-wood bed leg was found at Pompeii (Mols 1999, 81).

Willow

This appears to have been a wood used occasionally in cheap furniture, such as the couch of a peasant couple in Ovid's *Metamorphoses* (8.656). More use was made of the thin, supple branches for wickerwork (see below).

Oak

This is rarely mentioned in literature in connection with furniture, but was probably used extensively as a non-spectacular but sturdy material. Pliny, for example, lists an oak table veneered in citrus-wood (*Natural Histories*, 13.94). A fragment of an oak cupboard has been found in Britain, while tests revealed a bed leg and a cradle made of it at Herculaneum (Mols 1999, 79-80).

Other woods

The most common type of wood of those identified from the surviving wooden furniture found at Herculaneum is silver fir, used in almost every bed or couch tested, as well as for racks, a cupboard and a stool. Other woods identified in furniture include cypress for a round table and lime and olive for small chests (*ibid.,* 74, 76-81). Different woods could be used on the same piece of furniture, where woods suitable for turning such as box, hornbeam and beech were chosen for table legs and bed legs (*ibid.,* 74, fn 408; 80-1) while the more visible parts of the furniture, such as the table top, could be made of a wood with a more decorative colouring. Other woods would also have been used according to their local availability. In Britain fragments of an ash stool or table top (see *42*), an oak cupboard (see *6*), and chair/couch legs of beech, walnut, and oak have been found (Holmes and Raisen 2003, 131-2).

Wicker

Wickerwork was used extensively for high-backed chairs, in a variety of weave patterns. It was also occasionally used for stools and for hampers used in agriculture (Columella, *On Farming,* 11.11.90). Pliny records the use of white-coloured willow withies with the bark removed for chairs (*Natural Histories*, 16.68.174).

2 STONE

Marble

Three-legged tables, bench-tables and benches were made of marble, and could on occasion have very detailed, intricate carving. In Italy these items of furniture are usually found in 'public' spaces within domestic houses such as the *atrium* and the peristyle, and seem to have been used as indicators of the owner's status.

Other stone

In the provinces, local stones such as sandstone, Purbeck marble, and Bath stone were used for serving-tables and benches. Other items made in stone, such as tombstones and altars, were usually given a thin skin of white undercoat and were then painted, and it may be that some elements of stone furniture were also painted. Occasionally, solid masonry was also used, such as the external benches outside the front entrances of some houses in Italy; at least one masonry garden *triclinium* was covered in plaster and painted.

Shale

Shale is a type of stone, originally formed from compressed mud, that can be easily worked. Polished with oil, it has a shiny black finish like jet. It was used in Britain for making three-legged tables.

3 METAL

Bronze

Occasionally items of furniture such as three-legged tables, benches and foot-stools were made completely out of bronze. Sometimes bronze elements were made for composite items, like bronze legs of folding tables with marble or wooden tops, or the fittings on wooden couches. It is not clear how common such furniture was, as the large amounts of metal used in them made them prime candidates for being cut up for scrap.

Iron

Iron was not used extensively in furniture-making, apart from folding stools and folding chairs. It was sometimes also used, unseen, in beds and couches to form weight-bearing legs that were concealed beneath a more decorative exterior.

Silver and gold

While it is clear from literary evidence that furniture decorated with gold or with silver was known, it is not always certain whether they are talking of furniture that was made of the solid metal (only possible for small items not required to bear much weight), made with all-over plating, with plaques and appliqués or else covered with leaf or paint. As both metals are comparatively soft and not good for load-bearing furniture, most gold and silver furniture is likely to be simply decorated with the metals, although Elagabalus is said to have had 'couches made of solid silver for use in his dining-rooms and bedrooms' (*SHA Elagabalus,* 20.4) and Pliny mentions women using silver hip-baths (*Natural Histories,* 33.54.152).

Silver was certainly used for tables on occasions. During Trimalchio's feast described in the novel *Satyricon*, the guests are taken to a second dining-room to admire the treasures of their host's wife, including 'tables of solid silver' (Petronius, *Satyricon*, 73). The first-century treasure of Hildesheim included a silver leg either from a folding table or a tripod, while a fourth-century silver folding table, now heavily restored, was found at Polgárdi, Hungary. As currently displayed it is 114cm tall, with legs decorated with three-dimensional figures of cupids on dolphins, griffin-heads and nereids riding on tritons, as well as extensive beading and incised decoration (Kocsis and Tóth 2005, pl. 77).

4 BONE

Bone and ivory was usually used for decorative veneer rather than structural elements. The one exception was hinges for cupboards and chests which were made from cylinders of bone on a wooden core. This type of bone hinge has been found through out the Roman Empire.

5 DECORATION

Furniture decoration included the use of veneer, where a thin layer of one material is used to cover the whole of a cheaper base material below so that none of it is visible; appliqués, where decorative elements are stuck on top of the base material, leaving most of it still visible; and inlay, where one material is inset into the base material so that it lies flush with the surface, again leaving most of the base material still visible.

2 Part of the wood mosaic design from a bed with boards from Herculaneum (*after Mols 1999*)

Veneer

Wood

Pliny cynically describes veneering as a way of selling one tree many times over, but for many purchasers it was the only way they could afford expensive-looking furniture. He wrote: 'the principal woods for cutting into layers and for using as a veneer to cover other kinds of wood are citrus, turpentine-tree, varieties of maple, box, palm, holly, holm-oak, the root of the elder, and poplar. Also the alder ... supplies a tuberosity that can be cut into layers, as do the citrus and the maple.' He also mentions beech, larch, pine, and fir as being suitable for veneering (*Natural Histories*, 16.84.231; 16.84; 16.76; 16.82).

In many cases a veneer of one type of wood was used to give the illusion that the piece of furniture was made out of solid wood, as is common today. However, 'wood mosaics' were also used to decorate pieces of furniture, where the veneer was used to create a design. Small pieces of wood were cut to shape to form geometric patterns and while it is possible different woods were used to create coloured patterns, surviving examples all use the same wood (*2-3* and *colour plate 6*). Pliny mentions that strong-patterned grains, particularly a style of grain called 'fennel wood', were preferred for veneering, and on the surviving examples of wood mosaic found at Herculaneum, the effect relies on the contrast of the grain on neighbouring pieces of wood, and not on contrasting colours or wood types as on more modern marquetry. At Herculaneum, the wood veneer is *c*.1.5-2mm thick, deeper than modern veneers which are usually *c*.0.6mm due to modern cutting techniques (Mols 1999, 97).

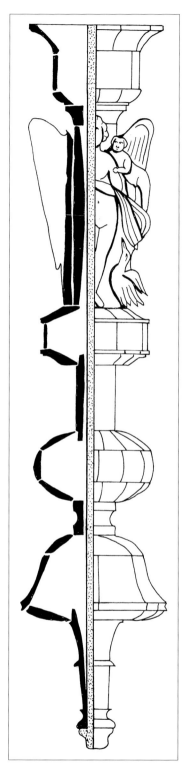

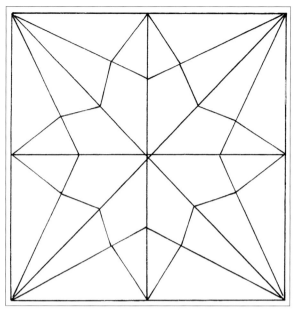

Above: 3 The wood mosaic pattern used on a stool from Herculaneum (*after Mols 1999*)

Left: 4 An ivory-veneered leg from a couch (*after St Clair 2003*). Central iron rod shown stippled

Ivory, bone and antler

Ivory was seen as an expensive luxury material, and bone as the cheaper alternative. However, ivory, bone and antler all have different qualities that make one or the other more suitable for use in certain ways, depending on requirements, and sometimes ivory and bone were used on the same object without distinction. While some furniture-makers may have passed bone off as ivory with purchasers unable to tell the difference, it is possible they may not have always cared anyway, as long as the result was a polished white finish. This concern for the finished effect over material can be compared with Roman 'jet' jewellery, which study has shown could be made of jet, shale, or cannel coal, and even black glass; the black shiny effect was of more importance than the material used. Study of ivory-veneered couches has shown that the workmanship on bone items could be just as good as that on ivory, and that the same workshop could work both bone and ivory (St Clair 2003, 14, 18).

Ivory and bone could be used to veneer wooden furniture, in particular couches, so that no wood was visible and the couch looked as if it was made of solid ivory. The legs were made with a central metal load-bearing pin concealed behind wooden decorative elements in the shape of large bell-shaped, spherical and drum-shaped components. The wood was then covered with carefully shaped, interlocking sections of ivory or bone glued or pegged into place. On some examples the plaques were fixed into position in an unfinished state, so that they could be smoothed down while *in situ* and then carved with relief decoration that continued seamlessly across the joins. Where deep relief was required the necessary thickness could be achieved by gluing together additional layers of ivory (St Clair 2003, 28).

An example of a couch dated to the first century BC or the first century AD now in the Fitzwilliam Museum, Cambridge, shows just how many different plaques could be needed, with over 120 pieces used on a single leg (4; Nicholls 1979). As well as the four highly decorated legs, there would be wide decorative panels along the sides of the frame with elaborate 3D carvings at each corner, and side panels on the *fulcrum* (pillow-rest).

Bronze

Early beds and couches often had elaborately-shaped legs that were designed to look as if they were made of solid bronze, but which in fact had only a thin cover of bronze sheet over wooden elements strung onto an iron weight-bearing core.

Other materials

Pliny mentions the use of animal horn, tusks, ivory and tortoise-shell as veneers on wood (*Natural Histories,* 16.84, 232). Martial describes a semi-circular dining-couch

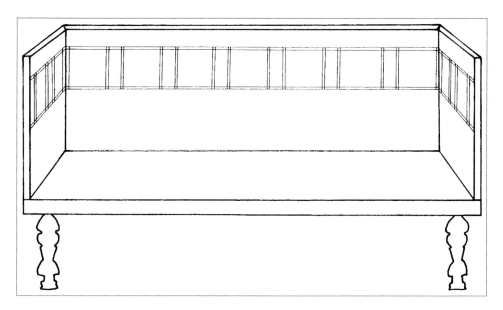

5 Reconstruction of a couch from Pompeii with bone appliqué or inlay decoration (*after Spinazzola 1953*)

decorated with crescents of tortoise-shell (*Epigrams*, 14.87); the material may well have been popular as its mottled pattern is reminiscent of the patterns of some wood burrs (*colour plate 7*).

Appliqués and inlay

Ivory and bone

Most ivory and bone was used as veneer, on top of the wood, without any of the wood being visible. There are, however, some examples of bone strips either attached to the wood or inlaid into it to create a contrast with the wood itself. Bone was used on a dining-couch from a villa at Boscoreale, and two beds with boards from the House of the Trojan Shrine and the House of the Ephebus in Pompeii had 'sticks' of bone forming geometric patterns while one cupboard had strips of bone on its doors and another had diamond-shaped bone inlay (5; Mols 1999, 106; fns 673-4).

A fragment of a fourth-century cupboard door from Hayton, East Yorkshire was made of oak with small bone plaques inlaid in the wood to form geometric patterns (6; Hartley *et al.* 2006, cat. no. 138). The patterns were created by cutting a wide groove for each of the lines of decoration, which were then infilled with both wood and bone plaques, so it is possible that the wood inlays were of a contrasting colour wood to the oak. Other examples of inlay are smaller: a griffin and a Bacchus bust on the legs of wooden tables from Herculaneum have eyes of inlaid ivory (Mols 1999, cat. nos 16, 18).

Bronze

First-century wooden beds and couches were often decorated with highly ornate bronze appliqués. These could be three-dimensional, such as the animal heads and human busts attached to the ends of *fulcra* (pillow-rests), or decorated strips attached to the front of the bed-frame. The bed with boards from the House of the Wooden Partition, Herculaneum, for example, had decorated copper alloy strips attached to the top edge of the boards that were decorated with palmettes inlaid in copper and probably also silver and niello (Mols 1999, cat. no. 1). Other loose strips have been found at Pompeii, with recessed panels and inlaid silver decoration in floral designs (Ward-Perkins and Claridge 1976, nos 183-5). Decorated strips were also used as corner brackets on beds and in particular dining-couches. They were used to strengthen the frame, but because they were visible, they were also decorated.

Silver

Pliny records that in the first century 'the beds of women have for a long time now been entirely covered in silver, and for a long time dining-couches (*triclinia*) as well' (*Natural Histories,* 33.51.144), and at Herculaneum a bed decorated with silver leaf decoration has been found, although it no longer survives (Mols 1999, 99). Pliny refers to side-boards and dining-couches in the Punic and the Delos styles decorated with silver, and says that before 82 BC there were supposed to be only two 'silver dining-couches (*triclinia*) at Rome' (*Natural Histories*, 33.51. 144-5).

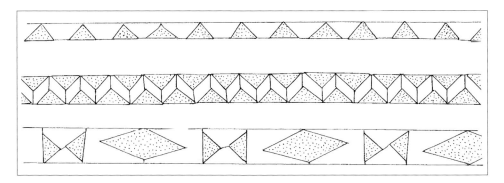

6 Pattern of wood and bone (stippled) inlay from a cupboard from Hayton, East Yorkshire (*after Hartley et al. 2006*)

Gold

Three gold dining-couches were displayed in the triumph of Pompey over Mithridates in 61 BC, and Pliny refers to dining-couches in the 'Punic fashion' decorated with gold (*Natural Histories*, 33.51.144), but generally the rich preferred to show their wealth through citrus-wood and ivory. Gold leaf or gilding was probably more common, and would have been available to a larger section of the population. Juvenal refers to a gilded bed belonging to a rich woman (*Satires*, 6.594), while surviving furniture from Italy includes a chest with 'gilded veneer' and a shrine with gilded capitals on wooden pillars, and even the carved supports of racks in the Gladiator's Training School in Pompeii had gold leaf decoration (Mols 1999, 99, 109).

Other materials

Examples of glass as inlay on marble tables have been found (Mols 1999, 110). Nero had travelling couches decorated with pearls (Pliny, *Natural Histories*, 37.6.17).

Paint

Pliny mentions tortoise-shell being painted to imitate the more expensive types of wood: 'high prices are sought for couches and orders are given to outdo turpentine wood, make a more costly citrus, and counterfeit maple' (*Natural Histories*, 16.84.233), but both wooden and stone furniture (including marble) might also have been painted in bright colours in their own right. Modern tastes prefer the natural appearance of wood and stone, but these were cheap materials to the Romans, and as they had a love of colour and pattern it is not surprising that they painted their furniture as well. The most common colour that has survived is red, which has been found on a bed, *biclinium*, cupboard, shrine and table. One bed from Herculaneum had geometric patterns in red while one from a villa at Boscoreale had bands of different colours over a red base. A door, either of a room or from a cupboard, had yellow and blue decoration (Mols 1999, 99).

CARE OF FURNITURE

Rough fish-skin was used in workshops to smooth and polish wood and ivory, although it is not clear if it was also used in domestic surroundings as well (Pliny, *Natural Histories*, 9.14.40; 13.34.108). Oils such as cedar oil, rose oil and juniper-berry oil were also used to polish wood, while the lees of olive oil (*amurca*) gave 'a high polish' (Mols 1999, 98; Cato, *On Farming* 98). Although there is no literary evidence to prove that wax was used as a polish, the overall number of references to household cleaning in Roman literature is low, and as it is known that Punic wax was used to protect wall paintings, it may also have been used to protect wood (Pliny, *Natural Histories*, 33, 40, 122). Also according to Pliny 'citrus-wood tables are best kept polished by rubbing them with a dry hand, especially just after a bath' (*Natural Histories*, 13.30.99).

3

Beds and couches

In richer households there would be beds used for sleeping in the bedrooms and couches for reclining on to eat in the dining-rooms, but in poorer houses the same piece of furniture would make do for both functions. Even in rich houses, where bedrooms were used as studies or places to hold meetings with important guests, beds could be used as day-time couches, so that the two terms are interchangeable in the Roman world. Although 'couch' has been used primarily to refer to furniture used for dining in the following chapters, there was never a sharp division between 'bed' and 'couch', and any comments about 'beds' also relate to 'couches' as well and *vice versa*. Beds were almost always made out of wood, although the parts not concealed by soft furnishings could be highly decorated to disguise the use of wood.

DESIGN

The basic design consisted of a rectangular base supported usually by four legs, typically connected by stretchers from front to back. Longer dining-couches may have had an extra supplementary pair of legs, which were usually undecorated even if the four main legs were highly decorated. The base could have either a wooden or rope lattice to support the mattress *(7)*. The wooden frameworks could be quite complex, such as the example from the House of the Wooden Partition, Herculaneum, which had three lengthwise and nine width-wise slats, with another framework of two stretchers connected by three ties below them to act as a strengthener to the bed-frame (Mols 1999, cat. no. 1). At Herculaneum, the location of the strengthening frame is sometimes associated with additional legs. A bed with straps from the House of the Two *Atria* in Herculaneum, now lost, had straps *c.*20cm wide stretched four times across its width (Mols 1999, 36),

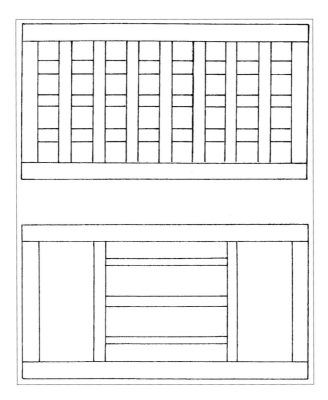

7 Typical couch mattress-support. Top: wooden lattice. Lower: 'gate' strengthener fixed to the bed-frame below the upper mattress-support

while images of beds carried by people cured by Jesus show a lattice of rope (see also Martial, *Epigrams*, 5.62.6; Petronius, *Satyricon*, 97). Both beds and dining-couches could have a pillow-rest (*fulcrum*) or a head board to one end, but could also have boards on two or all three sides.

Both beds with *fulcra* and with boards could have highly turned decorative legs, developed from an original Greek design. Beds with *fulcra* appear to have longer legs than beds with boards. Surviving legs from *fulcra* beds have lengths such as 36, 38 and 46cm to the top of the leg above the bed-frame (Steffanelli 1990, cat. nos 34, 36, 43, fig. nos 34–5), and the reconstructed ivory veneer leg is 48cm to the underside of the bed-frame (see 4; St Clair 2003, fig. 3.10). Images of beds with boards often show comparatively short legs, and a surviving leg from Herculaneum was only 32cm long to the underside of the bed-frame (Mols 1999, cat. no. 1). The legs had a structural iron rod for strength up the centre, which then had wooden rings threaded onto it of various shapes including drum and bell, often alternating between a narrow and a wide element. This was then covered with a copper alloy sheath that was purely decorative, or with bone veneer. The feet of the legs were not turned and often took the form of animal feet. On beds with *fulcra*, but not on beds with boards, the iron bar sometimes passes through the frame of the bed where it was hammered over and the end covered with a decorative mushroom-shaped copper alloy fitting. If a *fulcrum* was used, it sat on these terminals. As far as the evidence exists, the *fulcrum* was not fixed to the bed, the weight of the stand presumably being enough to stop it moving under the weight of a person leaning against it.

SIZE

At Herculaneum the surviving beds have a length between 2.04 - 2.22m and a width of 1.06 - 1.25m. A larger bed that no longer survives measured 2.45 x 1.44m. In some bedrooms, a niche was set into the wall to accommodate the bed, and a survey of these niches suggests an average bed size of 2.15 x 1.15m (Mols 1999, 38). Couches used for dining were well over 1m wide, as the diners generally reclined across the couch at an angle rather than along its length and they had to be wide enough to accommodate this. Couches that were used in living-rooms were also used for reclining, and not for sitting in the manner of a modern sofa. The narrowest width of the surviving beds and couches at Herculaneum is 1.06m, while the seat width of a modern sofa is in the range of 0.65m, so a Roman sitting upright on a couch would not have any back support if they wanted to keep their feet on the ground.

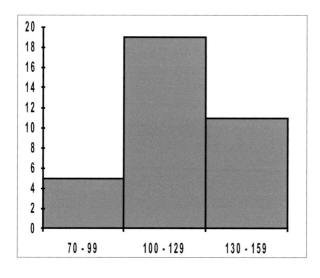

Graph 1: Width of 35 Roman beds in centimetres (*after Wallace-Hadrill 1991, fig. 10*)

The widths of beds varied considerably. Graph 1 shows the widths of a selection of 35 beds from Pompeii and Herculaneum collected by Wallace-Hadrill. For comparison, a small single bed is 75cm wide, and a more typical single 90cm (approximately 3 ft), a double is *c.*135cm wide, and king-size 150cm (approximately 5 ft). In this sample of Roman beds, the typical size of bed was somewhere between a modern single and double, but it is likely that in the ancient world, people did not expect to have as much space as modern sleepers (compare also the size of beds allowed for soldiers in the eighteenth century, 1.8 x 1.2m (6 x 4 ft), on the basis of two soldiers per bed, which gives 60cm per person (Douet 1998, 23; fig. 24)). People other than man and wife sharing a bed was as common in the ancient world as it has been in all periods up to the twentieth century. Pliny the Younger refers to a 'freedman, a man of some education, … sleeping in the same bed as his younger brother' (*Letters*, 7.27.12).

At Herculaneum there is a single example of a bed designed for a child, 1.2m long by 70cm wide (Mols 1999, cat. no. 3). It has no legs so must have rested on the floor, and has a low frame round it to help stop the child rolling out. How common such specially designed children's beds were is unclear, but it would only have been possible for the wealthy.

COUCHES WITH TURNED LEGS AND S-SHAPED PILLOW RESTS (*fulcra*)

Bronze-decorated wood

The *fulcrum* was a stand, roughly triangular in profile with a wide base tapering to a narrow top, which could be placed at the head of a bed to form a type of headboard or pillow-rest, sometimes with a second one at the other end (*8*; Mols 1999, 103). The stand itself was made of wood, but had elaborate bronze or bone decoration on the visible ends to match the decoration on the body of the bed. These could be highly decorated with busts, usually connected to Dionysius and Bacchus, such as Silenus or a cupid, or animals such as mule, horse, dog, duck, lion, panther or elephant (*9*). The bust, on a circular background, usually decorated the lower end of the *fulcrum*, and a twisting horse or mule head the narrow top-end.

The bronze plates, made up of three or four separate elements, were cast in high relief and were usually multi-coloured with plating or inlays of different metals. The three-dimensional animal head at the top could have inlaid white eyes, or the details of the wreath round its forehead and the animal skin round its neck picked out in gold-coloured brass or inlaid with silver decoration. At the other end of the plate the bust would have similar decoration. The central section consisted of a flat metal sheet surrounded by a raised frame that could be relatively

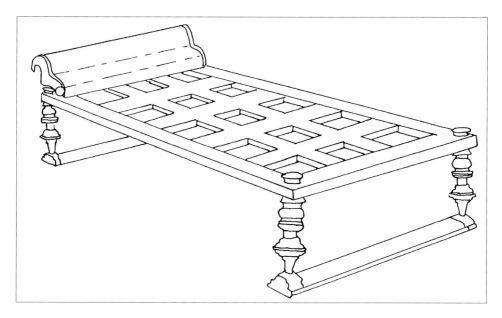

8 Typical design of a bed with *fulcrum*

9 Bronze *fulcra* from Italy. Top: left: from tomb at San Vittorino, Italy. Right: from Rome. Lower: left: unknown provenance, Naples Museum. Right: from tomb at Chieto, Italy

plain or decorated with moulded floral designs, sometimes picked out with brass. The flat plate was covered by scenes created by fine incised lines and rows of dots. The background was often brass-coloured, with the figures and vegetation picked out in silver with some details left in the same brown bronze colour as the frame. The long strips that decorated the bed-frame could be similarly moulded and decorated with silver and brass and the feet themselves sometimes had additional inlaid floral designs, although the legs themselves were left plain.

The couches with decorated bronze or ivory elements would have been very expensive items of furniture. This type of couch is widely known because of the large number of surviving bronze or ivory decorations which can be admired as works of art in their own right, but a fragment of a wooden *fulcrum* from a shipwreck that had been carved with a swan's head suggests cheaper all-wood examples were also known (Mols 1999, 106, fn 671). Reconstructions usually show beds with *fulcra* as single beds. If these were certainly single couches, they would have to have been used in the Greek style of dining, with a single person reclining along the length of the couch, rather than in the Roman fashion of three people to a couch, reclining across the width. Pliny says that this style of dining-couch with feet and *fulcra* of bronze first became fashionable at Delos (*Natural Histories*, 34.4.9), and were in use by the second century BC. The type went out of fashion before the end of the first century AD.

Ivory-decorated couches

A study made in 1984 identified at least 186 examples of couches covered in ivory or bone veneer dating to between the third century BC to mid-first century AD. This form of couch was copied from a Greek design and they were made only in the period when Hellenistic luxury goods were fashionable for the rich. When imitating Greek art went out of fashion, production seems to have ceased (St Clair 2003, 32-3). The couches were not intended to be wooden beds decorated with ivory elements, creating contrasting colours and textures, but were designed to look as if the bed was made of solid ivory. The ivory was highly carved with patterns as well as figures, usually with a connection to Bacchus (as with the bronze decorated examples).

Most of the known examples come from Central Italy, where they were probably made, but they seem to have been exported either as complete items or as loose collections of the more complex elements to be assembled at their destination, as examples have also been found in Germany and Gaul. In Gaul, they remained fashionable until the end of the first century, at least a generation after they had gone out of fashion in Italy (*ibid.*, 31-2).

Such a large number of examples have survived because they were used as funerary couches that were then burnt on cremation pyres, the surviving fragments being collected up and buried at the same time as the human remains. This could possibly mean they had a specialist role purely as funerary furniture, in which case the high level of workmanship that went into them made them an extreme example of conspicuous consumption. Their fine quality, however, suggest that they must have had a longer life than simply the few days necessary for the laying-out of the corpse and the funeral, but that for whatever reason, they were also considered suitable offerings for the dead.

BEDS WITH BOARDS

This term refers to a bed with wooden walls *c.*50-60cm high on two or three sides, which helped to protect those using it from damp walls and draughts. The walls could be vertical, curved in the lower section while vertical above, or could have a double curve (*5* and *10*). Examples are known from the early first century AD, but the type may well have been in use for some time previously (Mols 1999, 40). There are a number of surviving examples from Herculaneum, where they are found in rooms identified as bedroom, bedroom/study, living-room/study, and dining/rest-room. Some of them had a fully vertical wall which seem more often to be used as beds, and some had a curved lower section to the walls with a vertical section above which seem more often used as dining-couches, although there is no hard and fast rule due to the interchangeable functions of the bed/couch.

The boards could be decorated in a number of different ways. The most common type of decoration were panels, but examples at Herculaneum also have boards with complex wood mosaic veneer, decorated copper alloy strips along the top edge of the boards, strips of bone appliqués, egg-and-tongue moulding and painted geometric patterns (Mols 1999, 39; cat. nos 1, 9, 13). The decoration was only on the internal sides of the boards, as the external sides were rarely visible, as they were pushed up against walls on at least two sides. The sarcophagus from Simpelveld, Holland, shows a bed with boards decorated with geometric designs, with the end boards curved and set at an angle for the pillow (*colour plate 10*). The front edges of the end boards are carved into a shape reminiscent of a dolphin, an animal used on the head-board of frame beds (see below) and on the arms of desk chairs (see *37*).

The bed with boards decorated with wood mosaic from Herculaneum is a very fine example of the type. It was found in a small living-room/study in Insula Orientalis II, 10, where it occupied all of the back wall and approximately two-fifths of the room's length. Amongst other items found in the room were two bronze candelabra, 17 lamps, silver, bronze, glass and pottery vessels, a votive altar

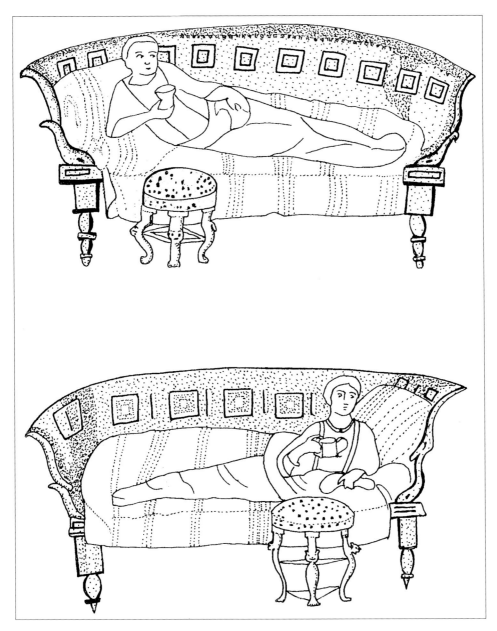

10 Mosaic from tomb at Henchir–Thyna, Tunisia, showing husband and wife reclining on couches with curved boards

and a box. The bed is almost 2m long and 1.06m wide and has boards on three sides made of planks glued together horizontally and then covered with wood veneer. The lower half of the boards are thickened to give the boards a slightly S–shaped profile from the side, while the top parts are vertical and decorated with moulding along the top edge. The wooden veneer is of an unknown wood, but is not the silver fir used for the bed-frame itself. The veneer takes the form of a complex meander above a line of rectangles on the vertical parts of the boards at a level high enough not to be concealed by the soft furnishings.

Another example from Herculaneum with boards only on two sides, had the end panel unusually set at an angle of *c.*120° to act as a headboard (Mols 1999, cat. no. 9). This was found in a ground floor room that has been identified as a bedroom/study, along with three wooden chests containing wax tablets.

FRAME BEDS

While *lectus* was the term used of beds in general, a second word, *grabatus*, was used of beds of a simpler construction than beds with *fulcra* or beds with boards. The term is used of the beds of the poor, beds found in lodgings and belonging to the sick and ill waiting to be cured by Jesus (Martial, *Epigrams* 12.32; Petronius, *Satyricon* 97; *Vulgate,* Mark 2.4). The type covers less elaborate beds, often with a delicate framework and generally a headboard at only one end. A large number of these beds are shown in late Roman Christian scenes depicting Jesus healing the sick, such as the paralysed man being lowered from the roof of a house, which are of great interest as they often show the beds without the mattress so that the details of webbing used to support the mattress are visible (*11*; cf Petronius, *Satyricon,* 97). In these images the webbing is often shown to be rope, although Diocletian's Edict of Maximum Prices also refers to linen bands (*11*).

A first-century bronze mirror from Italy shows a couple on a highly decorated bed with a single headboard (Johns 1982, pl. 35). The perspective of the bed is skewed so that as well as showing the side of the bed, the back of the headboard is also visible, which is decorated with a band with four niches containing figures. Unless this elaboration is artistic license, it suggests that this side of the head board was visible rather than more typically pushed up against the wall. The bed also has a bead-and-reel turned frame and decorative legs at the four corners plus two narrower legs between them on the short side, all four being joined by a stretcher at ground level. The mattress cover is also highly decorated.

This type of bed, although rarely quite so decorative, is depicted in a number of sexual scenes such as those shown on oil-lamps (*ibid.*, figs 115-6) and wall paintings from Pompeii. The beds in the wall paintings from one brothel (VII, 12, 18) are brown in colour with plain frames, four legs at either end with outer decorated legs and inner plain ones. Some headboards appear to be straight, while others curve out slightly at the top, and most have two panels, side by side (Cantarella 1999, 84, 88, 89). At least two examples have low footboards, half the

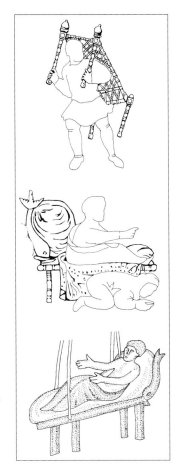

Right: 11 Frame beds. Top: man carrying a frame bed with rope mattress-support. Ivory relief, Andrews Diptych, Victoria and Albert Museum. Middle: frame bed with dolphin headboard. Ivory relief from casket, British Museum. Lower: frame bed with dolphin headboard. Mosaic, St Apollinare Nuovo, Ravenna

Below: 12 Bed with headboard and foot-stool. Wall painting from building VII, 12 18, Pompeii

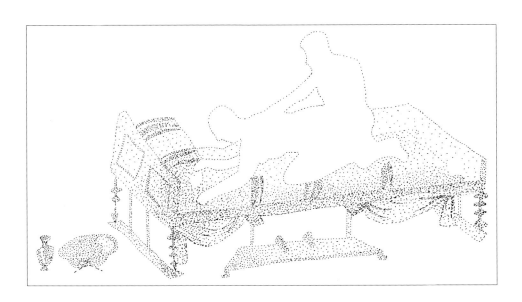

13 Model of a frame bed from a child's grave, Hawara, Egypt

height of the headboard, although this design appears to be relatively uncommon (*12*). Similar scenes from other buildings show beds with elaborate legs but no headboards (*ibid.*, 98).

A model of a modern-looking frame bed found in a late second century grave at Hawara, Egypt has a vertical head board consisting of two stretchers between two upright posts and a mattress support of spaced slats set in grooves within the bed-frame (*13*; Walker and Bierbrier 1997, no. 322). A fourth-century decorated glass bowl shows a bed with another upright head-board (Wietzmann 1979, 401), but there appears to be an increasing fashion (or increase of images) of beds with gently curved headboards, either with an elaborate S-shape, such as that shown on a fifth-century ivory plaque from Rome (*ibid.*, no. 407), or an early fourth-century wall painting of Jacob resting on his bed (*ibid.*, no. 419).

An elaborate version of the curved headboard has the side members carved into the shape of a dolphin, head down and tail in the air, a form also used on beds with boards and desk chairs (*37, colour plate 24*). One dolphin headboard is shown on a mid-third-century oil lamp from Athens (Johns 1982, fig. 90), but they become more common in the later Roman period when beds become common in art because used in illustrations of biblical stories. A sixth-century mosaic in the Basilica of St Apollinare Nuovo at Ravenna shows a man being lowered from a roof by his friends, and an early fifth-century ivory casket plaque from Rome, now in the British Museum, shows Peter resurrecting Tabitha as she rests on a similar bed (*11*). The bed frame of this example has timbers with a circular cross-section and heavy lathe-turned decoration. The legs are not set at the very end of the frame, so the terminals are decorated with a knob, while the headboard is set at a slight angle and the dolphin comes complete with a trilobate tail at the top. A bed shown on the mid-fifth-century Andrews diptych has even more elaborately turned bed-frame, and in this example the rope lattice used to support the mattress is clearly visible. The rope can also been seen on the bed carried on the back of a cured man in another of the mosaics from St Apollinare Nuovo. The bed itself has a simple headboard with two spacers, while the legs at the foot have uprights that rise above the framework ((Bustacchini undated, 109, fig. 3). All the examples cited have been single beds, although this is no doubt no more than an artistic convention. Only a fourth-century North African pottery dish shows the healed man carrying a bed with the dimensions of a double, which takes up much of the available space in the small image (Wietzmann 1979, 402).

MASONRY BEDS

Wall paintings in one of the brothels in Pompeii (VII, 12, 18) show couples on wooden beds with headboards, with bedroom items such as a footstool, wash-bowl and jug, or candelabrum nearby (*11*). The reality in the brothel itself was not so elegant. Solid masonry bases the width of the cramped rooms took up half the available space. Often one end had a quarter-rounded moulding to act as a pillow-rest (*14*; Cantarella 1999, 87, 88). With a cloth concealing the masonry base, as used on some wooden beds, a thick mattress and pillows, masonry beds need not have been either ugly or uncomfortable. Masonry bases were, after all, used by the wealthy for outside *triclinia* (*colour plate 12*). However, interior masonry beds seem to be most frequently found in rooms identified as brothels or in slave-quarters.

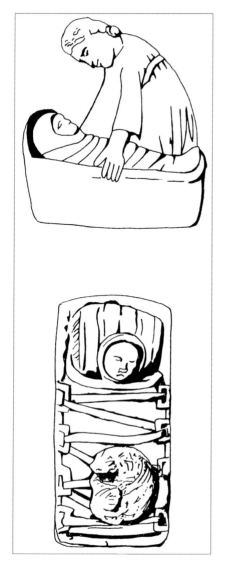

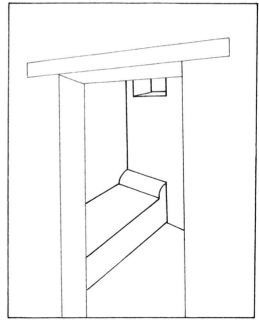

Above: 14 Masonry bed base, in brothel at Pompeii

Left: 15 Top: nurse with a baby in a cradle. Relief from tombstone, Cologne. Lower: baby strapped to a board. Stone relief, Nuits, France

CRADLE (*cuna* OR *cunabula*)

The first-century physician Soranus, in his book on women's health, gives details of the preferred bedding to be provided for babies. He advises that a new born infant should not be put on anything too hard or too soft, and should be laid 'for instance, upon a pillow filled with flock or, otherwise, with soft hay; and the mattress should be hollowed-out like a channel, so that the newborn when put down should not roll about. And the little head should be placed in a somewhat raised position, on which account some people, not unreasonably, permit bedding in troughs which have been made up as beds. The coverlets should be warmer or thinner according to the season, and what lies underneath should be aired and changed piece by piece, so as not to chill the newborn nor to make it full of evil smell. This is why some people have also strewn sweet bay or myrtle leaves underneath to give a sweet smell.' He goes on to recommend that the child should not sleep in the same bed as the mother, in case she rolls on top of it, but suggests that the cradle should stand near the bed, or even on the bed itself (*Gynaecology* 2, 10[30].16[85]; 2.17[37].37[106], trans. Temkin 1956). Roman art shows two forms of cradle; rocking, usually made of wood, and non-rocking, more often made from basketwork, although Soranus gives ways of rocking the non-rocking forms 'by suspending the cradle, or by balancing it upon diagonally opposed stones' (*ibid.*, 2.17[37].40[109]).

Rocking

Martial refers to a male slave or freedman rocking his cradle when he was a baby (*Epigrams*, 11.39), and an example of a rocking cradle has survived from Herculaneum (Mols 1999, cat. no. 11). It has a wooden frame-work with stretchers on all four sides to stop the baby falling out, connected to two slightly curved rockers. It was found in a living-room rather than a bedroom, and still had the skeleton of a baby within it, but as six other skeletons were also found sheltering in the same room, it is probable the cradle had been carried in from some other room when the group decided to gather together in one place. A sixth-century copy of the Bible, the *Vienna Genesis*, shows a child in a similar wooden cradle, but with the lower part of the sides solid and only one stretcher above (*colour plate 9*).

Non-rocking

A third-century tombstone of a wet nurse from Cologne shows her putting her charge to bed in a cradle. In this example, the baby was heavily swaddled as was common in the ancient world. Sometimes the baby was tied down onto a wooden board, although Soranus warns against the practise (2.9[29].14[83]; 2.10[30].16[85]). An example from Nuits, France shows a baby with a pillow and a blanket, and a dog asleep at its feet, the child being held immobile by large straps running diagonally across its body (*15*).

4
Dining-couches

Although the typical method of Roman dining is represented as being nine people reclining on couches round a central table, this was only for those who could afford a large, separate dining-room and who had guests to entertain. Breakfast, and other minor meals where there were no guests, were informal, and sometimes did not even require a table (Seneca, *Letters to Lucilius*, 83; trans. Phillips Barker 1932). Otherwise, they were probably taken sitting on stools and chairs round a dining-table, and if there were no guests for the main meal of the day and only a few family members dining, it is likely that a single couch and upright chairs in a room other than the dining-room were used. Plutarch observed that 'when a rich man dines alone with his wife or intimates he lets his tables of citrus-wood and golden beakers rest in peace and uses common furnishings' (*Moralia*, On Love of Wealth, 528).

A Roman social evening took place in the dining-room, with the entertainment continuing in the same room after the tables had been cleared away. As the guests spent so much of their time in the dining-room, the couches were often designed to impress, with decorated bronze, gold or silver fittings or elaborate woodwork, or were covered with expensive coloured mattress-covers and cushions. Pliny describes the escalating use of precious metals on dining-couches as people attempted to out-do each other in luxury, which could explain why dining-couches made up a large percentage of the luxury goods Verres was said to have plundered while governor of Sicily (Pliny, *Natural Histories*, 33.51.144; 33.52.146; 37.6.12-4; Cicero, *Against Verres*, 2.2.74; 2.4.26).

The designs of couches are as for beds, with the most long-lasting and wide-spread form being the bed with boards.

16 Relief of *triclinium* with 12 diners from Sentinum, Italy

Triclinium

One of the Latin names for a dining-room, *triclinium,* was a transference from the word for the layout used in classical dining that consisted of three couches set round a central table. No wooden *triclinium* has survived from the ancient world, but at Herculaneum two of the surviving dining couches are *biclinia*, made as a single item with two arms forming an L-shape, and *triclinia* may sometimes have been made in a similar way, although three separate couches pushed together as one would have been more convenient for moving. The Herculaneum *biclinia* consist of beds with boards, and it is possible some *triclinia* were also made this way, but surviving images of *triclinia* tend not to show any backs to the couches (*16*). It is easier to get on and off a couch without disturbing the diners to either side by going feet first over the back of the couch rather than having to swing the feet over the front of the couch.

Reclining to eat was a fashion borrowed from the Greeks, but as with most such borrowings the Romans altered it to suit their own needs. In Greece there were an uneven number of couches, usually 7, 9 or 11, with only one or two people per couch lying along its length, and a separate table for each couch. In Rome, the typical-dining room had three couches in an inverted U-shape, with shared table(s). In smaller *triclinia* only a single, central table was needed, but in the later, larger versions, multiple tables would have been required. In the early period, three people shared each couch, so that a typical dinner party was nine (in comparison, the most common size of modern dining-table usually seats six).

The three diners reclined across the width of the couch, probably slightly diagonally, which therefore had to be at least *c*.1.25m wide to accommodate them. The diners reclined on their left arms, supported by cushions or the mattress, leaving their right arm free to reach for the food and drink. One of Plutarch's after-dinner conversation pieces discusses why there seemed to be a lack of space at the beginning of a meal, and ample space later: 'In general, each guest, while eating, assumes a posture almost flat, since he must stretch his right hand forward to the table; but after eating he turns back more on his side, forming a sharper angle with the couch and occupying no longer a flat surface, but merely, one might say, a line … so each of us takes up space at the beginning of a meal by leaning forward to face the table but later changes position on the couch so as to occupy more space vertically than horizontally. Most of our company, however, found the answer to the question in the settling of the cushions as they are crushed by the weight of the diners; they flatten and spread like old shoes' (Plutarch, *Moralia*, Table talk 5, question 6, 679-80).

The couch at the back was called the *lectus medius*, the couch to the left (when entering the room) the *lectus imus* and the couch to the right the *lectus summus*. The *lectus imus* was used by the family of the house, and the other two by the guests, with the guests, in theory, carefully placed according to status. The place of honour for the most important guest was at the left hand end of the middle couch, next to the host who sat on the far end of the *lectus imus*. Not all meals would have been so formal; Plutarch records a meal hosted by his brother where he told his guests to choose their own seats, although a late-arriving guest of status refused to stay when he saw the place of honour had not been left for him (*Moralia*, Table talk 1, question 2, 1).

From the second century, but most common from the third century onwards, there was a tendency for the *triclinium* to sit more than nine diners. The best evidence for this change comes from mosaic floors where a U-shape of relatively plain mosaic covers the area for the couches and a T-shape of more elaborate mosaic covers the space left for the tables and across the service/entertainment end of the room (*17*). A study of some of the external *triclinia* of Pompeii designed for nine people shows that just under 0.8m were allowed per diner on the couches. The mosaics in the dining-rooms at Cabra, Spain, and the House of the Months, El Djem, suggest couches long enough for approximately 15 diners. The fourth-century Commanding Officer's house at Arbeia did not boast mosaics, but even here the couch area was marked out in cheap flagstones

17 Dining-room floors showing the location of the dining-couches marked out by the floor decoration. Left: Cabra, Spain. Middle: El Djem, Tunisia. Right: Arbeia Roman Fort, South Shields

while the rest of the floor was mortar/tile flooring (*opus signinum*). The length of the paved areas suggests they should also take 15 diners, and experimentation with reconstructed dining-couches has shown that they can indeed take 15 comfortably.

Biclinium

In houses without the space, or the need, for a full-sized *triclinium*, a *biclinium* could be used to accommodate four people comfortably (or six at a push: the presence of the boards on two or three sides means there is less available space for the diners' legs than the back-less *triclinium*, making it more cramped). As the name suggests, this was made up of two couches, set in an L-shape. At the House in *Craticum* in Herculaneum, the couches dominated the room, occupying the length of the entire east wall of the room, and two-thirds of the south wall (Mols 1999, cat. no. 5), with a large window opposite them overlooking the courtyard. The room also contained a marble table, a small wall cupboard, and a wooden cupboard containing glass and pottery vessels set against the south wall beyond the foot of the couch. In this example the two wings of the *biclinium* have boards on all three sides, even though it appears to have been made as a single structure rather than be two couches pushed together. The original height of the board separating the two couches is unclear, but it may well have been as tall as the back and other end board (53cm+), creating a barrier between two of the diners. When viewed from the front, the projecting arm of the *biclinium* is to the right-hand side, and is of the same length as the other arm. At the House of the Alcove in Herculaneum the equal-armed *biclinium* was also made as one, but here there seems to have been no board separating the two arms (Mols 1999, cat. no. 6). In

49

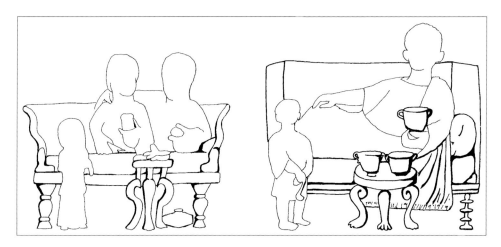

18 Left: bed with curved boards, tombstone of Aelia Aeliana, York. Right: bed with straight boards, tombstone, Cologne

19 Couch from tombstone of Victor. © *Arbeia Roman Fort (Tyne and Wear Museums)*

this room the couches were set about 30cm from the north and west walls, with a sliding door in the east wall overlooking the courtyard. When entering the room through the sliding door, the couch takes up most of the back wall, and has the projecting arm on the right-hand side.

Length	Width	Board height (m)
2.4	1.25	
2.4	1.25	0.56+
2.2	1.20	
2.8	1.10	
2.3	1.10	

Table 1: Dimensions of existing biclinia couches (Mols 1999, cat. nos 5-6)

Couches on tombstones in the north-west provinces

Scenes of meals are a common motif on tombstones in many parts of the Empire, including the north-west provinces. Some show the deceased reclining, usually alone, on the couch accompanied by incidental people, such as a slave, who were often depicted at a smaller scale. Others show groups of people round a central table, with no one figure pre-eminent. On scenes from France and Germany with groups of people dining, the details of the couches are usually lost behind the seated women and the table in front. Reclining on the couches is reserved for men in these scenes, and two or three men share the couch.

Most examples from Britain depict beds with curved boards on three sides and legs shown as rather simple balusters, while in Germany there is a preference for showing upright boards and legs consisting of drums spaced along a narrow-diameter upright (*18*). These might reflect genuine regional or chronological fashions, but are just as likely to represent local stone-masons' artistic styles. The tombstone of Victor at South Shields certainly seems to reflect the use of a 'pattern-book' design (i.e. copied from another sculpture rather than directly from life), although modified with local detail. The stone-mason almost certainly came from Syria, and the couch is very similar in design to those shown on tombstones at Palmyra. The Palmyrene examples have recessed strip decoration between each corner of the bed-frame, fluted decoration on the legs, and a decorated mattress cover, all of which are echoed on Victor's tombstone, although in this case the fluted decoration on the legs has become incised lines. The Palmyrene couches have legs with terminals above the bed frames, and some include depictions of *fulcra*. Victor's couch has the more typical Romano-British curved boards at head and foot (the back board probably having been missed out altogether), but the stone-mason has made them no higher than the cushion, probably to make the couch look like those normally shown on Palmyrene tombstones (*19*; cf *22*).

A few tombstones show more than one person reclining, such as the tombstone of Aelia Aeliana from York, but most suggest the couches were designed to accommodate a single person, who is always shown reclining along its length, in contrast to the traditional Roman method of dining by lying across the couch. The presence of a three-legged dining-table and slaves serving drinks show these were supposed to be taken as dining scenes, but this probably does not reflect actual contemporary practise. The image of a man reclining on a couch has a very long history, and the Roman versions are very clearly copied from Greek art. In Greece, men are always shown drinking rather than eating since this was the important part of the evening's entertainment for them (unlike with the Romans when the meal was the focus of the evening's entertainment) and they are shown reclining along the length of a couch designed for one person, as this was their style even for banquets with multiple guests. These features survive into the Roman versions of the scene depicted on tombstones, and it is likely the image became so standardised as an image that no Roman ever considered what scene was actually being represented (Dunbabin 2003, 106-8).

Some of the communal eating scenes from Germany probably give a better idea of the form of dining for non-banquet meals, when either no guests have been invited, or only close friends. Two or three men recline on a couch, and an equal number of women sit in chairs around a single table. The Igel Monument from Germany shows one such scene, with two men reclining on a couch and two women sitting in chairs, being served by at least two slaves (*26*). The scene is only a minor image on the monument, but it is an image the family were happy to present publicly, and a family that could afford a 23m high monument with over 22 carved scenes was not exactly poor. All the reliefs show every-day events, including slaves doing the washing up, rents being paid and goods being transported, rather than the more leisure-based activities of the rich such as banquets, baths or hunting, and presumably reflect accurate scenes.

External triclinium

Dining-couches were built in open-ended rooms or gardens of town-houses, inns, hotels and vineyards in parts of the Empire where hot weather made dining outside a pleasure. At Pompeii 53 masonry *triclinia*, three wooden *triclinia*, five masonry *biclinia* and one semi-circular couch (*stibadium*) have been recognised so far (Jashemski 1979, 36, n. 1), although the number of wooden examples is almost certainly under-representative. The external couches were sometimes sheltered by the branches of nearby large trees, but more often had a wooden framework overhead covered by a vine or similar plant, supported by wooden posts or masonry pillars (Jashemski 1979, figs 145, 249-50).

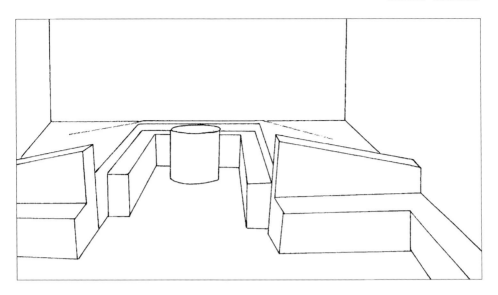

20 Masonry *triclinium* from the House of the *Cryptoporticus*, Pompeii. Note sloping couches, the ledge on the inner side of the couches and the benches in front of the couches

The masonry examples are generally equal-armed, although occasionally the *lectus imus* (family couch) is slighter longer. The solid bases generally have a sloping top, slightly higher at the front edge than the back, which is a feature not seen on the wooden couches used internally (*colour plate 12*). Some of the bases have small niches set in the front for storage. The external *triclinia* also often have a ledge along the front of the couches; sometimes this is just a ledge cut into the front edge, while on others it is about half the height of the front of the couches (Jashemski 1979, figs 143, 145). The deeper ones may have been steps up onto the couches, while the higher ones may have been resting places for cups.

Another difference with the internal dining arrangements is the fact that the central table is also made of masonry and therefore not moveable like the light-weight three-legged tables used inside. There is only one central table, which can be circular, square or rectangular, and is usually a solid block of masonry, although the circular examples are more likely to have a marble top set on a narrower base. One table, in Orchard I.22, had an ornamental panel of marble set on the top of the masonry base (*ibid.,* figs 371-2). There was generally the base of another table set just beyond the end of one of the couches, usually the *lectus summus* (guest couch). This may have been a serving-table, or may sometimes have been used for cooking.

The *triclinium* at House of the *Crytoporticus* has many of these features. The couch has a ledge round the front, while the side couches have head rests on the short ends and a low bench for children to sit on. There is a single central table and a serving-table to one side (*20*).

A few of the masonry couches were decorated with painted plaster or marble panels, but many may have been left plain, being hidden by drapery. All of them would have required mattresses and cushions. The more elaborate examples included water features nearby or incorporated into the structure itself such as fountains, water jets set in the table and waterfalls. At the House of Octavius Quartio (II.2.2) the dishes of food would have floated in the water basin between the couches, a conceit also used by Pliny at one of his villas (Dunbabin 1991, 124).

Semi-circular couch (stibadium *or* sigma)

The name *sigma* came from the Greek letter C, used to describe the semi-circular shape of the cushion or couch. The semi-circular couch was used with a single, central dining-table, like the *triclinium*, but with the added advantage that the shape meant that every-one was the same distance from the table. They were in use from the first century, as a masonry base for a garden example from Pompeii (House VIII.3.15) shows, but it was not until the early third century that they became increasingly popular. By the fourth or fifth century they had become more common than the rectangular couches (Dunbabin 1991, 130-1). The idea for a semi-circular couch may have developed from the long cushion curved into a semi-circular shape that was used for outdoor picnics, where the diners sat on the ground and merely propped themselves up on the cushion (*ibid.*, figs 28-30). A mosaic from Piazza Armerina shows hunters in the field reclining on such a cushion, but similar picnics also took place in the cities. Septimius Severus, before he became Emperor, bought some elaborate gardens and took 'frugal' meals with his children, 'reclining on the earth' (SHA *Severus,* 4.6).

By the late second or early third century, the increasing popularity of semi-circular couches can be seen in the number of dining-room mosaics being designed with them in mind; they also came to influence the design of the room itself. As a semi-circular couch set in a rectangular room left unused corner space behind the couches, dining rooms were increasingly made semi-circular (apsidal) in shape to match.

Literary evidence suggests that between five and eight guests were the preferred number for dining on semi-circular couches (Dunbabin 1991, 143, n. 59). Martial mentions one that held eight, and on another occasion talks about inviting an extra guest so that six would not be dining on a *sigma* designed for seven (*Epigrams*, 10.48.6; 14.87). The smaller numbers of diners are a contrast to the fashion for increased numbers of guests that could be accommodated in the large rectangular dining-rooms of the third and fourth centuries. However, larger dining-rooms for *stibadia* could have separate apses for extra sets of semi-circular couches, providing more flexibility in the number of guests that could be invited, although at the cost of a loss of intimacy as the distances between the

21 *Stibadia*. Top: scene from the *Vienna Genesis,* showing
the most important diner at the left-hand end of the semi-
circular dining couch. Middle: women dining, with the guest
of honour sitting in the central position. Ivory box, Egypt.
Lower: couch with three-legged dining-table and water-
heater. Mosaic, Sepphoris, Israel

apses would not encourage cross-conversation. An extreme example, the House
of Bacchus at Cuicul, had a room with seven apses for approximately 50 guests.

The place of honour for the most important guests was originally in the centre,
but later it seems to have moved to one end of the couch (Sidonius, *Letters*, 1.11). A
mosaic from the sixth-century Basilica of St Apollinare Nuovo, Ravenna showing
the Last Supper taking place on a *stibadium* has Jesus sitting on the left-hand end
when looking towards the couch from the front. When looking at the couch in
this way, a diner on the right-hand end of the couch reclining on his left arm as
usual had his back to the entertainment, but faced the other guests; the diner on
the left-hand side had a good view of the entertainment but his back to the other
guests. When the place of honour was on the left-hand side, the host no longer sat
beside the guest of honour but on the opposite end of the couch.

The Ravenna Last Supper scene shows the wooden ends of the couch
decorated with four panels, and a scene on an ivory box from Egypt shows
pillars and swags on the ends of the couch (*21*). Martial talks of a couch 'inlaid
with crescent tortoiseshell' (*Epigrams*, 10.48.6), suggesting the couches could be as
highly decorated as *triclinia*. Other images show the wooden frame totally covered
by drapery. There are no clear images of a *stibadia w*ith boards at the back.

5

Soft furnishings for beds and couches

As the Romans did not always distinguish between a bed for sleeping and a couch for reclining, modern terms like 'pillow' and 'cushion' imply a precision not reflected in Latin. Some words also cover more variations than would be acceptable now, such as cloaks that were also used as blankets (*sagum*), and fabrics that could be blankets, coverlets, curtains or hangings (*tapete, stragulum*).

MATTRESS AND PILLOW STUFFING

Literary evidence

When Varro discussed the derivation of the word for 'bed' in his work *On the Latin Language*, he explained that in the past people first made beds of piles of straw and grass to raise themselves off the ground (5.166). Juvenal also talks about the distant past as 'the era when a chilly cave provided a tiny home, enclosing a hearth, the household gods, the herd and its owners in communal gloom, when a mountain wife made her woodland bed from leaves and straw and the furs of her neighbours, the beasts' (*Satires*, 6.5). Varro suggests that the next development was to cover the loose bedding with coverings (*segestria*) of wheat stalks (*seges*), before people moved on to stuffed mattresses (*On the Latin Language,* 5.166).

The word for mattress was *culcita*, that Varro incorrectly interprets as coming from a word meaning to force in, stuff, or pack, since 'chaff or stuffing or other stuff' was forced into a mattress (*ibid.,* 5.167). Mattresses stuffed with types of grass continued to be used by poor people, as the filling could be collected for free. The poor couple visited by Jupiter and Mercury in Ovid's *Metamorphoses* had 'soft sedge grass' in their mattress (8, 655), while Horace describes a 79-year-old miser 'lying on a straw bed (*stramentum*), even though rich coverlets moulder away in a chest' (*Satires*, 2.3.117). Both Varro and Pliny make a point of noting that soldiers in forts also continued to use straw for their beds in their own time (Varro, *On the Latin Language*, 5.166; Pliny, *Natural Histories,* 8.73.193). Martial wrote a gift-tag for hay to be used to 'let your crackling mattress swell, cheating your mule' and one for 'chopped-up marsh grass' that was called Circus stuffing, because this was supposed to be the stuffing used in cushions on the seats of the poor in the Circus (*Epigrams*, 14.162; 14.160). Pliny mentions that in Spain 'country people use esparto grass for bedding (*strata*), for fuel and torches, for shoes and for shepherds' clothes', while the tufts from the top of reeds 'serve instead of feathers in the bedding of innkeepers' (*Natural Histories*, 19.7.27; 16.64.159). The cradle found at Herculaneum contained remnants of textile and leaves (of unspecified type) which may have come from the mattress stuffing (Mols 1999, cat. no. 11).

The next step up in comfort was to use raw wool as stuffing. Martial refers several times to wool stuffing from the Leuconicus tribe in Gaul, including a gift-tag for 'Leuconican Stuffing. Are the bed strappings too close when you press down on a feather mattress? Accept fleeces shorn for the thick cloaks of soldiers' (*Epigrams,* 14.159; see also 11.21.8; 11.56.9). Pliny says that the use of fleece as stuffing, in this case fleeces originally used by metal-polishers, originated in Gaul (*Natural Histories,* 8.73.192) as did the use of linen: 'the linen grown by the Cadurci people has especial fame for use in mattresses; the use of it for this, and likewise as a stuffing, is a Gallic invention' (19.2.13), suggesting that the sack of the mattress was made of linen.

The most expensive type of stuffing was feathers, as it was the most comfortable, providing the mattress was well-stuffed. In Pliny's discussion of white geese, he explains that: 'in some places they are plucked twice a year, and clothe themselves again with a feather coat. The plumage closest to the body is softer, and that from Germany most esteemed. The geese there are a bright white, but smaller … the price of their feathers is five *denarii* per pound. And owing to this, Commanding Officers of auxiliary troops frequently get into trouble for having sent whole cohorts away from outpost duty to capture these birds; and luxury has advanced to such a pitch that now not even the male neck can endure to be without goose-feather bedding' (10.27.53-4). Martial wrote a gift tag for swan's down: 'When tired, rest on feathers of Amyclae which the swan's inner down has given you' (*Epigrams,* 14.161), although cheaper sorts of feathers were also used, as mentioned in Diocletian's Edict of Maximum Prices. For the very rich, other fanciful stuffings could be demanded. The Emperor Elagabalus 'could not rest easily on mattresses that were not stuffed with rabbit fur or the feathers from under the wings of partridges, and he moreover used to change mattresses frequently' (*SHA,* 19.9).

The late second-century writer Clement of Alexandria warned people against the dangers of feather beds in his book of instruction for the lifestyle of Christians, *The Instructor*. After explaining that luxurious bed-clothes should be resisted, he continued on to the mattresses beneath them. 'For beside the reproach of voluptuousness, sleeping on down is injurious when our bodies fall down as into a yawning hollow, on account of the softness of the bedding. For they are not convenient for sleepers turning in them, on account of the bed rising into a hill on either side of the body'. His argument was that soft beds burnt up energy, while harder beds allowed the proper digestion of food; soft beds encouraged total and enervating relaxation, while Christians should be ready to wake at a moment's notice (2.9).

There are a couple of references to sweet-smelling stuffings, although it is not clear how common this practise was. Pliny recorded that 'mint is pleasing for stuffing, and pervades the tables with its scents at country feasts' (*Natural Histories*, 19. 57.160), while Cicero condemns Verres for riding in a litter 'which contained a cushion of transparent cloth from Malta stuffed with roses,' following the custom of the old kings of Bithynia (*Against Verres*, 2.5.11.27).

Inflated cushions

A biographer of Elagabalus records a practical joke carried out by the Emperor: 'Some of his humbler friends he would recline on air-cushions and let the air out while they were dining, so that often the diners were suddenly found under the table …. He was the first to think of placing a semi-circular cushion on the ground instead of on couches, with the purpose of having the air-cushions deflated by slaves who stood at the feet of the guests and thus let the air out' (*SHA Elagabalus*, 25). How common such cushions were is uncertain, but air-filled balls were a well-known type used in the exercise yards of the baths, and the point of the story is the practical joke, not the novelty of the cushions (Martial, *Epigrams*, 4.19).

Archaeological evidence

Excavations in Colchester have revealed a 'bed' carbonised in the fire that destroyed the town when it was sacked by Boudicca in AD60/61. It may have been no more than two mattresses stacked on top of each other in the corner of a room since little wood suitable for a framework was found in the area. Rope found underneath the lower mattress may have been part of the springing of such a framework, if it existed, but it was clear that the lower mattress sat on or very near the floor long before the fire (Crummy 1984, 44). The two mattresses were twice as long as they were wide (1.92m by 0.97m). Both were made of a diamond twill cloth with remains of at least two fabrics in fine and medium-fine weave lying on top. Some of the cloths, including the mattress covers, appear to be wool, but the remains of stuffing could not be identified (Wild 1984, 45).

BLANKETS, BEDSPREADS AND COVERLETS

Literary evidence

Varro says that the material used to cover a mattress was called a *stragulum*, from a word meaning 'to cover' (*On the Latin Language*, 5.167). According to Roman law, *stragula* should be considered under the heading of clothing rather than furniture (*Digest*, 33.5), and the word is sometimes combined with the word for 'clothes', as when Pliny lists the signs of impending death, including 'making folds in the bed-covers (*stragulae vestis*)' (*Natural Histories,* 7.52.171). The word often seems to be quite a general, non-specific term, including both the modern meanings of 'bed-clothes' and 'throws'. Diocletian's Edict of Maximum Prices mentions lengths of linen cloth for use on beds, which were presumably used as sheets/mattress covers. Literature suggests that both blankets and more decorative counterpanes were used over the top of them.

Juvenal refers to a snow-white linen Cardurcum coverlet from (or in the style of) the Gallic tribe (*Satires*, 7.221; see also 6.537), and although the Romans considered wearing furs to be a habit only suitable for barbarians, they did not seem to have any prejudice against fur or skin blankets in the bedroom. Pliny mentions 'bedroom covers (*stragula*)' made of mole skins (*Natural Histories*, 8.83.226), Varro refers to *reno*, reindeer skin from Gaul or Germany and *gaunaca*, an Eastern fur prepared from weasel or mouse skin, and Augustine contrasts the luxury of a feather mattress and goat-skin coverlet with a simple mat for a bed (*Against Faustus the Manichean*, 5.5). However, wool with a raised nap is the most common material mentioned for bed coverings.

Martial wrote a gift tag for a type of cloth with a thick nap on one side for use in the bedroom, described as a 'shaggy covering (*stragula*)' (*Epigrams*, 14.147 and 152). Another gift tag indicates that a counterpane (*lodix*) could be used above the blankets: 'Counterpane. In case the coverings (*stragula*) are exposed on your bare bed, we joined sisters [two pieces of cloth sewn together] have come to you' (*Epigrams*, 14.148). These outer covers are often described as being shaggy (Pliny mentions that 'the coarse hair of a shaggy fleece has a very ancient popularity for *tapete; Natural Histories,* 8.73.191), and a reference by Ammianus Marcellinus implies a thick but not luxurious covering when he records that the Emperor Julianus 'always got up, not from feather bed nor silk bed-clothes of iridescent brilliance, but from thick covers (*tapete*) and hide coverings (*sisyra*) which the simple common people call *susurna*' (16.5.5).

Other references show that the these thick covers could also be colourful and highly decorated. The 'shaggy cloth' could 'glow with purple figured cloth', presumably in the form of a border or stripes (Martial, *Epigrams*, 14.147), while others had more extensive decoration; Martial also wrote of a 'many-threaded bedroom covering. The land of Memphis gives this gift to you; the needle of Babylon is now defeated by the weaving comb of the Nile' (*Epigrams*, 14.150). The implication is that the Egyptians could now weave figured cloth that was just as ornate as the multi-coloured, figured embroidery for which Babylon was famous. Ballio, a pimp in the play *Pseudolus* by Plautus, threatens his slaves with a beating 'til [your flanks are] perfectly polychrome, make 'em more colourful than Campanian coverings (*peristromata*) or Alexandrian clipped thick covers (*tappetia*) decorated with beasts' (1.2.14).

Clement of Alexandria urged his Christian readers to 'have the strength to banish magnificent bedding, gold-woven pillows, bed-clothes with an alternating smooth and golden pattern, dyed with shellfish purple, or made up from athlete's wraps, and the most expensive Eastern fur, and poet's mantles of purple, and soft and luxurious clothes, and beds softer than sleep' (*The Instructor*, 2.3). It is interesting that even this list of expensive bedding includes clothes in the form of athlete's wraps and poet's cloaks. The reindeer skins and fur mentioned by Varro as being used on beds were also used as cloaks, and are in a section about bed-clothes along with the *sagum*, a thick cloak preferred by soldiers, and *amphimallum*, a woollen cloth with a nap on both sides (*On the Latin Language*, 5, 167). Cloaks and blankets were often seen as interchangeable, as both were simply rectangles of thick woollen cloth. Martial also refers to a poor man using a toga on his beds (*Epigrams*, 11.56, 6). The poor who could not afford the gold-woven pillows and multi-coloured cloths decorated with figures made do with a blanket or two, which could also be used as clothing when necessary.

Diocletian's Edict of Maximum Prices

In AD 301, the Emperor Diocletian published an Edict establishing the maximum prices to be charged for a wide range of goods and services (Graser 1975; Erim and Reynolds 1970). The Edict was inscribed on stone panels in major cities throughout the empire, and fragments of versions both in Latin and translated into Greek have survived. There are a number of sections on bedding, some of which were included in the lists of clothing which mainly survive in the Greek versions of the text. The lists give quality, quantity and price in *denarii*. In the following selection, some of the sections have been re-ordered and the quantities/prices adjusted to be more easily comparable, and a selection of wages taken from the Edict has been included for comparison with the cost of the bed-clothes. The translations are based on Graser 1975 and Erim and Reynolds 1970.

7 For wages		*denarii*
Shepherd, with maintenance	1 day	20
Farm worker, with maintenance	1 day	25

Fine-work joiner, with maintenance	1 day	50
Baker, with maintenance	1 day	50
Figure painter, with maintenance	1 day	150
Teacher of arithmetic, per pupil	1 month	75
Teacher of public speaking, per pupil	1 month	250
Advocate, for pleading a case	per case	1000

18   For down

Goose down	1 lb	100
Down of different birds	1 lb	50
Willow(?) wool or down	1 lb	10
Stuffing or wool flock	1 lb	8
2nd quality	1 lb	4
Soft feathers of various birds	1 lb	2
Cushioning of reed tufts (?)	1 lb	1

Inflation has increased the cost of goose feather from five *denarii* per pound in the first century (as revealed by Pliny) to 100 *denarii* in the early fourth century. In the Edict, goose feather is 10 times the cost of wool stuffing and 50 times the cost of the cheapest bird feather.

19   Covers

Thick spread for a couch, single	4500
Thick spread, Cappadocian or Pontic	3000
Wrap for a couch, white, weighing 12 lb, best quality	2500
Thick spread, Cappadocian or Pontic, 2nd quality	2000
Thick spread, Egyptian	1750
Thick spread, African	1500
Wrap, ordinary, weighing 10 lbs	500

Dyed wrap (*endromida*), Arabian or Damescene
or any other kind, is to be sold at a price in which the
weight of the wool and the value of the embroidery,
have been included.

Covers (*stragula*) are to be sold according to the
value of the weight of the wool and the dyeing and
the embroidery.

Three different words are used in this section, which also includes lists of cloaks, capes and tunics. In the Greek text, a word for a 'thick spread' is used, sometimes translated from the Greek as 'carpet' (in the Edict, the word is also used for a cover for a horse). Also used is the word for a 'wrap', more often used to describe a warm mantle used by athletes or bathers to keep warm after exercise (but also used in the Edict to describe cloth to be used as a tent). The word used in a surviving Latin text is the general term for cover, *stragula*. Some of the items listed, not being qualified as certainly for furniture, may therefore have had other uses.

28   Bed linens

First quality

from Scythopolis	missing	
from Tarsus	missing	
from Laodiceia	missing	
from Tarsus, Alexandrian	missing	
Second quality		
(sub-divisions as above)	missing	
Third quality		
(sub-divisions as above)	missing	
From Laodiceia	1 web	5250
Bed linens which are inferior to the above 3rd quality		
1st quality	1 web	3000
2nd quality	1 web	2500
3rd quality	1 web	1750
Of coarse linen for the use of country people or slaves		
1st quality	1 web	1750
2nd quality	1 web	1000
3rd quality	1 web	800

Webbing

First quality, of linen, from Scythopolis, or Tarsus, or Byblus, or Laodiceia, or of any other purest linen	webbing	1700
2nd quality	webbing	1500
3rd quality	webbing	1400
Those that are inferior to the above 3rd quality		
1st quality	webbing	750

2nd quality	webbing	500
3rd quality	webbing	400

Of coarse linen for the use of country people
and slaves

1st quality	webbing	300
2nd quality	webbing	200
3rd quality	webbing	150

Mattress case (*culcita*; although in the Greek
versions this is translated as 'cushion')

from Tralles or Antinoe	2750

From Damascus or Cyprus and other places

1st quality	1750
2nd quality	1250
3rd quality	800

Linen which is inferior to the above 3rd quality

1st quality	600
2nd quality	500
3rd quality	400

Of coarse linen for the use of country people
or slaves

1st quality	350
2nd quality	300
3rd quality	250
Pillow case (*pulvinus*) for the use of country people	100

This section includes both mattress covers and 'bed linens', suggesting the bed linens may have been sheets used under blankets or bed covers. The webbing is that used on the wooden bed-frame to support the mattress.

The section takes the form also used in other sections of the Edict with sub-divisions of the cloth according to the place of manufacture, usually in descending order of cost, in five different qualities; first to third, inferior to third, and 'for country people and slaves'. For the bed linens, this provides 18 separate categories of cost, although unfortunately the prices for the more expensive items have been lost. For both webbing and mattress cases, where all the prices survive, the top of the range is roughly 11 times more expensive than the cheapest.

The bed linens are priced per 'web', the piece of cloth produced on a loom (although the exact size of this would be dependant on the size of the loom used), while the woollen cloths of the covers are priced according to their weight. The cheapest available soft furnishings for a bed, consisting of a stuffed mattress, pillow, bed linens and a thick cover, would work out in the region of 1660 *denarii*, approximately a month's wages for a joiner making fine furniture.

Artistic evidence

Mattress and pillow covers are frequently shown as being striped (*10* and *12*). Where the images are coloured, such as wall paintings from Pompeii, white or other pale colours are usual for the main colour of the cloth, with well-spaced stripes of a second colour, commonly red, running across the width of the mattress and down the length of the pillow. Other colours used include mid-green with red stripes and pale blue with dark red stripes (Cantarella 1999, 89, 93). The form of the stripes can take a variety of forms, from single lines, a thick stripe flanked by either one or two thinner stripes or groups of three equal-width stripes (Cantarella 1999, 55, 75, 99). In most cases the mattress and pillow are shown as being made from the same material, but occasionally pillows are shown in a different colour.

Some bed-frames were covered by cloths that reached the ground and concealed the whole frame, and others with slightly shorter cloths that revealed at least some of the ornate legs (Cantarella 1999, 55, 95). There are examples both of the cloth being the same colour as the mattress and of it being a contrasting colour. A mid-blue drapery with a yellow stripe round its lower edge was used under a red-striped mattress in a wall painting in the House of the Centenary, Pompeii and a white cloth with dark red stripes and another with golden-brown stripes were used under mattresses and pillows of pale blue with dark red stripes (Cantarella 1999, 55, 93, 95).

Other bed-frames were decorated with a cloth arranged in careful folds, either as one large swag or two smaller swags, with the tail-ends of the cloth hanging down vertically at either end just to the inner side of the bed legs in order to leave them exposed (see *12*). The ornate bed depicted on the back of a bronze mirror from Italy also has a vertical tail of cloth in the centre, between two swags (Johns 1982, pl. 35). This arrangement of cloth on the bed often has the appearance of being attached to the side or underside of the bed-frame, rather than being draped over the whole of it and then arranged in artistic folds. The decorative bed-frame on the mirror back is not concealed by the cloth, and on a wall-painting from Pompeii, the dark brown of the bed-frame is visible between the pale blue of the mattress and the tan of the draped cloth (Cantarella 1999, 137). This style of draping the bed-frame has the advantage of requiring less cloth, which was always expensive in the Roman period.

DINING–COUCH COVERS

Literary evidence

One of the most important actions in preparing a dining-room for a meal was to cover the couch mattresses with a decorative cloth. In the play *Stichus* by Plautus, the slave Stephanium records that she 'was summoned here from home a while ago, for after they had word of their husbands coming, we've all been on the jump there, covering couches, getting things tidied up' (Plautus, *Stichus,* 5.3.675; cf 2.2.357), and even a poor peasant couple presented by two unexpected guests 'threw a drapery over [the couch] which they were not accustomed to bring out except on feast days … it was a cheap thing and well-worn, a very good match for the willow couch' (Ovid, *Metamorphoses*, 8. 657-9). When Horace invites a friend to dinner, he offers him 'no untidy couch-cover, no spoiled napkin to make you wrinkle up your nose' (*Letters*, 1.5.22), and in one of his *Satires* he warns against allowing unwashed couch-covers to defile expensive Tyrian purple cloth (2.4.84).

Due to the cost of cloth in the ancient world, the length of material wide and long enough to cover three couches could be hugely expensive, and they would have been safely stored away until needed. The cloth would be equally as important in indicating the owner's wealth as any of the metal fittings or other decoration on the wooden frame of the couch. Pliny mentions some Babylonian covers (of multi-coloured tapestry or embroidery) that had been sold for 800,000 *sesterces* in the past, which had recently cost the Emperor Nero four million *sesterces;* elsewhere Pliny mentions that just 400,000 *sesterces* would buy a 15 hectare (37 acres) vineyard (*Natural Histories*, 9.63.137; 14.5.48).

Purple couch-covers are mentioned as a form of short-hand for wealth, as when Martial refers to some-one sleeping 'on feathers and a purple couch' or when he talks of a 'brand-new purple cloth draping your couch' (*Epigrams*, 12.17.8; 11.56.10). In Horace's story of the town and country mouse, the vision of a rich man's house included scarlet and purple cloths on ivory couches (*Satires*, 2.6101-4). In the first century AD Pliny quotes Cornelius Nepos, who says that when double-dyed Tyrian purple was first used as an edging for a toga in 63BC, it was disapproved of, but 'who does not use this purple for couch-covers (*triclinaria*) now-a-days?' (*Natural Histories*, 8.74.196).

Ammianus Marcellinus describes a banquet in the fourth century where 'the purple borders of the linen couch-covers were so very broad that the skill of the attendants made them seem all one piece', although in this case the owners were ruined by a joking suggestion that the purple edgings could be used to make an Imperial cloak (16.8.8). Other covers were decorated with human figures and complex scenes. In Petronius' fictional description of Trimalchio's banquet, the couch-covers were changed mid-meal to suit a course of game: 'the attendants came and spread over the couches coverlets ornamented with nets and men lying in wait with hunting spears, and all the instruments of the hunt' (*Satyricon*, 40). In a poem written while waiting for a banquet to begin, the fifth-century Sidonius refers to a similar motif, involving covers of red linen and purple wool and 'foreign' furnishings showing a Parthian on horseback shooting an arrow back towards animals shown running over hills (*Letters*, 9.113.14-32).

Artistic evidence

Couches used for multiple diners usually show the whole structure covered in cloth. A well-known wall painting of a party scene from Pompeii shows the couches covered by a yellow cloth decorated with two brown lines round the edge (Grant 1979, 47), while another, lesser known image of a dinner party has the couches concealed below light blue drapery with an orange/brown band round the edge (Dosi and Schnell 1986, 71). An image of Dido and Aeneas dining in the fifth-century *Vergilius Romanus* manuscript shows a *stibadium* covered in purple drapery, with a single, elongated cushion for the use of all the diners in white with red stripes and a fringe. The Queen also seems to have a supplementary cushion under her elbow decorated with red dots on white (Dunbabin 2003, pl.16). As these are fictional characters, it is impossible to say if the scene reflects contemporary practise or just long-lived artistic convention; the purple is short-hand for wealth, and wall paintings from the House of the Chaste Lovers, Pompeii, probably based on Hellenistic originals, show diners with red and white striped cushions (*ibid.*, pls 1-2).

Individual couches being used for dining generally show the mattress without loose drapery over it, although some German tombstones show a small fringed cloth over part (*18*). Colour images of couches unsurprising show the same type of colours as used on beds; a wall painting from Ostia shows a green mattress cover with red stripes (*colour plate 16*). The tombstones of Palmyra often show the mattress cover as being more highly decorated (*22*). The most common design is a plain cover (with the stylised folds that are a distinctive feature of Palmyrene textile sculpture) with a number of spaced ornate bands running across the width. These probably represent tapestry-woven bands rather than embroidery, since surviving examples of decorated cloth, either from covers or clothes, are almost always examples of complex designs being woven into the cloth whilst on the loom. The most common number of bands shown on the sculpture is three, but four and five are also known. The bands, often of a floral pattern with beaded borders, can all be of the same design or of alternating designs. Occasionally, two mattresses are shown on the couches, in which case the upper one is always shown covered by an all-over geometric pattern made up of rosettes or flowers

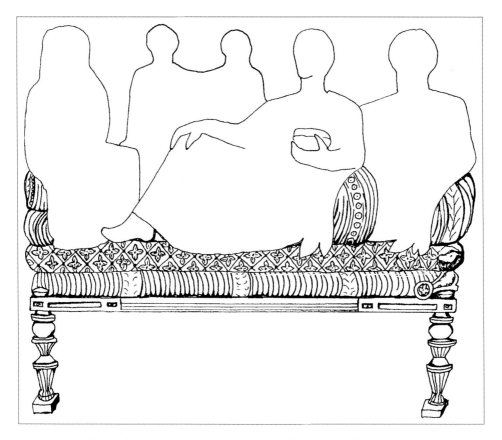

22 Bed with *fulcrum* at head end and two mattresses. Relief from tomb of Malkû, Palmyra

in squares. These covers are never shown with the multiple folds of the banded covers, but this may simply be because the artists did not want the complication of showing decorated cloth in folds, rather than because they were of a different fabric to the banded covers (Colledge 1976, pls 61-2, 69, 100-2).

Archaeological evidence

As it is often difficult to assign an exact function to a surviving textile, these are discussed in Chapter 12 with the curtains and hangings.

6

Dining-, serving- and display-tables

DINING–TABLES

On those occasions when Romans sat up to eat, they did not sit at a tall table in the modern western fashion, but ate at tables that were approximately the same height as their seats. They therefore could not get their legs under the table but could only sit with their knees up to it (*16; colour plate 12*). The table was often a small circular table of the same type that was used in more formal dining for when guests were invited, which meant reclining to eat with the table set in front of couches. Reclining leaves only one hand free and requires the table to be no further away than an outstretched hand. The tables were generally small, and were unable to hold many dishes at the same time, so this form of dining required the presence of slaves; first to cut up the food into pieces suitable for eating single-handed, and then to keep the small tables supplied with food either brought straight from the kitchen or a brazier in a nearby corridor, or from larger serving-tables elsewhere in the room. Dining-tables were always made of wood and were small enough to be portable. Some hosts had new tables brought in with a new course, and had all the tables removed after the eating had finished. In a modern dining-room, the large table is the most important piece of furniture in the room, but in the Roman world, it was the couches that were of greater importance. Although rectangular dining-tables were occasionally used in the provinces, the dining-table was traditionally circular.

Three-legged dining-tables

Wood
The three-legged circular table, also known as the Delphic table, came from the Greeks but was adopted enthusiastically by the Romans sometime in the second

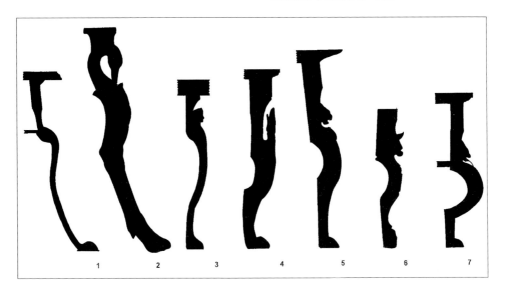

23 Profiles of dining-table legs (to common scale). 1, 3-5, 7: wood, from Herculaneum. 2: wood, with gilt decoration, from Egypt. 6: shale, from Colliton Park, Dorset

century BC and remained fashionable until the late Roman period. It was by far the most common form of Roman table, used throughout the Empire. It had a circular top, and three curved legs which could take a variety of styles, connected by stretchers to provide stability (*23; colour plate 11*). A number of examples surviving at Herculaneum provide details of their typical size. The heights are relatively similar, approximately 60cm, but the diameters of the table tops range from 42 to 61cm.

The table top could be decorated with mouldings on the edge that could either increase or decrease the size of the top surface (cf Mols 1999, cat. nos 14, 17-9; 15). The top of the table leg, where it joined the table top, tended to be vertical, and it was usually here that the legs were joined by stretchers. These were of even length and met in the centre, where a lathe-turned cap covered a central peg. The legs then curved out into a bow before returning to either a straight or slightly splayed leg.

The original Greek design had elegantly shaped but undecorated legs (as seen, for example, in the dining scenes from the House of the Chaste Lovers, Pompeii; Dunbabin 2003, pl. 1), and although the Roman versions usually added an animal head to the bow, plain examples are occasionally seen. One of the examples from Herculaneum had a plain leg leading up to the bow decorated only with a spiral carved onto one side (Mols 1999, cat. no. 15). The plain variation is also frequently seen on tombstones from the north-west provinces, where the legs of the tables have the characteristic bowed shape, which sometimes appears noticeably bulbous when viewed from the front, but rarely have any animal motif (*18*). Table legs made of shale decorated with griffins show that this motif was known and used in Britain, so the lack of animal designs on the tombstones may simply be the result of artistic convention. The stone-mason may perhaps have not been interested in including such a level of detail, or, due to the coarseness of the stone, simply not capable of it.

The majority of three-legged tables had an animal head at the top of the bow, sometimes emerging from acanthus leaves. Lion-heads and griffins are very common, but panthers and birds including swan are also known, as are dogs 'running' up the leg, and occasionally even a human head (*23*). The lower part of the leg and the foot are often realistically carved as an animal's leg, but can also be a more stylised general 'animal' paw. Where recognisable, they are most often a lion or a dog's paw, but panther, cow, horse, deer and antelope have also been identified.

An unusual three-legged table with a crescent-shaped rather than circular top has survived at Herculaneum that also has a rare male bust, possibly Bacchus, in place of the more typical animal head (Mols 1999, cat. no. 16). It is only 36cm in length and has a maximum width of 28cm, so Mols has suggested it may have been designed as an extension table to be fitted against a normal circular table, or possibly for use against a pillar as a side-table.

As dining-tables were seen by guests, they could be made of expensive woods, the epitome being a citrus-wood top with ivory legs. Martial compares a table belonging to a friend with his own, which was made of beech and propped up by a pot sherd, while elsewhere a gift-tag apologises for a maple table because not only was it not made of citrus it was not even made out of veined wood (*Epigrams*, 2.43; 14.90). One of the surviving examples from Herculaneum has legs of box-wood and a walnut top, while a leg from another is made from hornbeam, which may have come from another table made of two contrasting woods (Mols 1999, cat. nos 15, 17).

Wall-paintings from Pompeii based on Hellenistic originals usually show the tables holding silver or glass drinking vessels, with no more than three or four to a table. This portrayed use of the table reflects the typical Greek use of this type of table, as in the Greek world wine-drinking was more important than the food. Roman banquet scenes sometimes also show a drinking cup or two on the table but often show dishes of food instead. One from Ostia has a complete fowl, a circular loaf of bread and a possible chop and another has a fish set on a dish larger than the table-top itself (Dunbabin 2003, figs 67-8). A banquet scene in the *Vergilius Romanus* from the story of Dido and Aeneas also shows a complete fish on a large dish, and three much smaller dishes, one for each diner (Weitzmann 1977, pl. 13). In contrast, in Germany and France, bowls of fruit are frequently depicted (*25*; Espérandieu 1965, nos 5146, 5154).

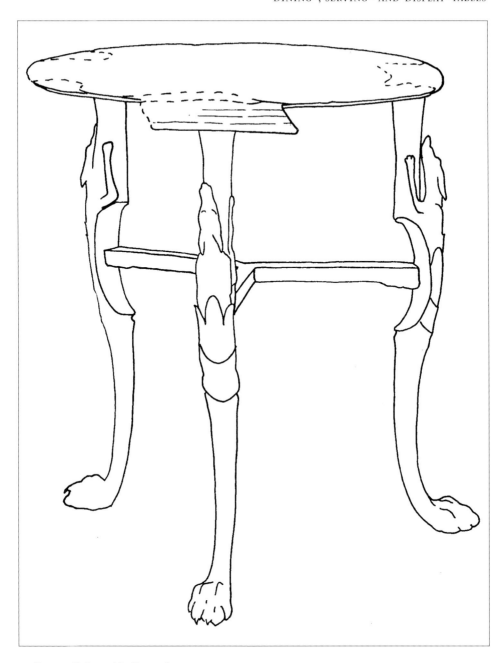

24 Bronze dining-table. Pompeii

Metal

Tables made completely from bronze were sometimes used, such as a complete example found at Pompeii (*24*). It is unclear how common these were.

Shale

In Britain there was a fashion for three-legged tables in shale. Fragments from at least 14 legs and seven possible table-tops have been recovered, mainly in south-west Britain close to the shale working industries at Kimmeridge Bay, Dorset. The earliest known date for these tables comes from a leg fragment found in a context dated AD 210-40.

A particularly elegant example survives from Colliton Park in Dorset (*23*, no. 6), carved with an animal that can perhaps be identified as a griffin (Liversidge 1955, 42). Instead of the usual band of foliage there is a band of fluted decoration on the bow, while the leg ends in an elegant claw. Similar heads with large, forward pointing ears and open mouths are found on a number of other leg fragments, which suggests a single workshop style (*ibid.*, pl. 46-8, 51-2). Other fragments were much plainer in design.

Two fragments of circular tabletops were recovered from Silchester. They are 17mm thick, with a wide rim thickened on the underside to accommodate the mortises cut into them to take the tenons of the legs. The larger example has eight concentric rings on the upper surface, but much more elaborate decoration on the lower face of the rim (identified as such because of the presence of the mortises), including beading, concentric rings and incised circles, chevrons and hatching. This time-consuming decoration would not have been visible on the finished table, and no convincing explanation can be made for it. If the discs are not tabletops, it is unclear what else they could be (Lawson 1976, nos 94-5).

Folding tables with straight legs

The late fifth-century ivory diptych of Probianus appears to show a folding Delphic table, with a circular top and cross bracing between the three (visible) legs. More common are the depictions of folding tables with straight legs on tombstones from the north-west provinces (*25*). They have rectangular cross-section legs decorated with two vertical grooves and a slightly expanded, out-turned foot. The thick legs suggest these were made of wood rather than metal, but the bracing was more likely to have been made of metal. This design appears on examples from Neumagen (Espérandieu 1965, nos 5146, 5155), Cologne (*ibid.* no. 6492), Arlon (*ibid.*, 4041), and Bonn (Horn 1987, Abb. 184). The tombstone of C. Iulius Maternus from Cologne shows an example without cross bracing, which is either a fixed version of the table, or the cross bracing has been missed out (*25*, lower).

One-legged dining-table

There is a rare example of a circular dining-table with a single leg, undecorated and tapering towards the top, depicted on a tombstone showing a man reclining on a couch (Espérandieu 1965, no. 71). Now in France, it is of unknown provenance

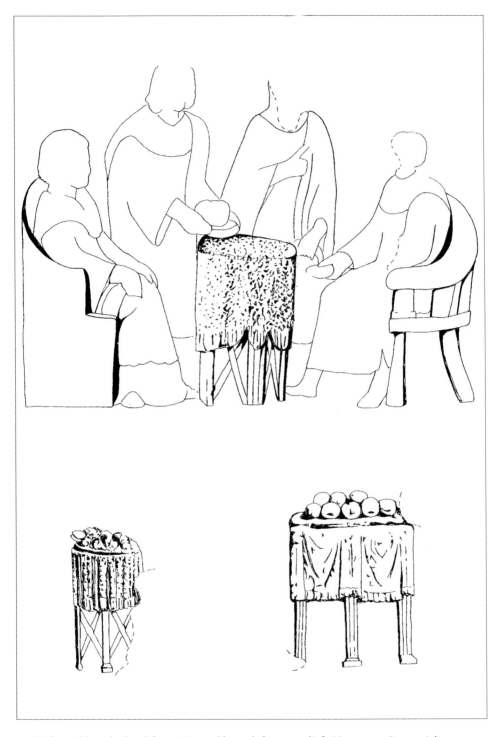

25 Folding table and related forms. Top and lower left: stone reliefs, Neumagen. Lower right: stone relief, Cologne

but the stone has a Greek inscription and a Syrian or Alexandrine provenance has been suggested for it, and perhaps reflects a local provincial fashion.

Rectangular dining-tables

Low

Although the Greeks used low rectangular dining-tables with dining couches, the Romans in the Mediterranean region preferred circular tables. In the northwest provinces, however, there is a sequence of tombstones showing a local fashion amongst the rich for rectangular tables (*26*). These are always shown draped in a table-cloth, so the details of the tables' construction is unclear, for although some appear to have solid sides, it may simply be that the table-cloth reaches down to a low-set stretcher, as visible on the scene from Neumagen (Espérandieu 1965, no. 5154). An example from France show three men reclining on a couch with curved boards, with a rectangular table set with three dishes of food, including a fish (*ibid.*, no. 5839), while other scenes show dishes of fruits (*ibid.*, nos 7806, 5154).

Tall

In the Mediterranean region, rectangular tables were sometimes used in taverns by people sitting up to drink or eat (usually an indication of the lower classes), although it is not always clear if the tables are only as tall as the seats or tall enough for the diners to get their legs under the table in the modern way (see *74*; Veyne 1987, 190). All the tables show low stretchers between the legs, making this a potentially uncomfortable way of dining.

Two images have been taken as showing that this way of dining became a widespread fashion in the late Roman period, indicating a general shift away from dining on couches to sitting up to eat. One is a sixth-century mosaic in the Presbytery of the Basilica of St Vitale, Ravenna, showing a biblical scene of three angels sitting at a table set up outside a building under an oak tree (*27*). The three guests already have a loaf of bread each laid on the table, while Abraham is coming out of the house carrying a meat course served on a dish. The table is rectangular, with upper and lower stretchers between the legs; the angels rest their feet on the lower one, although the artist has created a maze of bars in his confusion of perspective. It is possible that all three share a single iron bench, but it seems more likely they are each sitting on a folding stool. Red cushions are visible under the two end figures and to the right a grey frame and leg are visible (see Chapter 8 for other late Roman iron folding stools with red cushions). The dining takes place out of doors and the scene is mythological, both of which limits its relevance for every day dining practises.

26 Diners using a rectangular dining-table. Igel Monument, Germany

27 Diners using a tall, rectangular dining-table. Mosaic, San Vitale, Ravenna

The other example comes from a fragmentary fifth-century mosaic from Carthage (*28*). There are at least seven tables, and were probably originally at least two more. All of the tables seat three diners on one side of the table (presumably only an artistic device to avoid a cluttered scene), and there are numerous slaves carrying trays of food as well as a number of entertainers in the middle, including a pipe player and two dancing women playing a form of castanets. The tables are long and rectangular with low stretchers. The diners appear to be sitting on a settle, with a shoulder-high, solid wooden back. To avoid too many confusing lines, the artist has not shown the lower half of the diners' bodies below the level of the table, nor any of the seats' legs, and has also joined the seats' back to the tables.

This is almost certainly a depiction of a public banquet given by the owner of the house in which the mosaic was found. Public banquets (with or without additional cash gifts) could be given to mark a range of events such as religious ceremonies, anniversaries or funerals, and could be confined to just high-ranking town officials or to large numbers of local people up to and including the entire population of a town, and were often held outside or in large public buildings such as theatres and porticoes. If the banquet was given to a large number of people, it could be divided up by rank, with the rich reclining to eat and receiving more money while the lower classes sat to eat or were simply given hand-outs of food (Dunbabin 2003, 82-3, 92; fig. 45). The number of diners at each table in the Carthage mosaic, and the fact they are set out in an oval all looking inwards, probably reflects the unusual nature of the meal that would again not necessarily reflect normal eating practises (*ibid.*, 90-1). It is likely that sitting up to eat at rectangular tables was acceptable throughout the Roman period for 'public' dining, such as in taverns and at large public banquets, whilst reclining to eat remained popular for the higher classes in the east up to the seventh century.

Tables for stibadia

The standard three-legged dining-table was used with the semi-circular dining couch (*stibadium*), but a number of other table types were also used, including other circular tables with straight legs and drum-like tables (Dunbabin 2003, pls 13-4, fig. 116). Some tables were clearly designed as part of a suite with the couch, such as the circular table with solid sides and short legs which has the same decoration as the couch ends, shown in a scene of women dining carved on an ivory box from Egypt (see *21*).

The form of the couch led to the development of D-shaped tables, which often filled the whole available space in the inner curve resulting in the guests and serving slaves having to approach the couch from the rear (Dunbabin 2003, figs 118-9). Two D-shaped tables with a marble top and wooden base were found *in situ* in the House of the Stag, Apamea, Syria that was destroyed in the late sixth

28 Diners sitting on settles behind tall rectangular dining tables. Detail of mosaic, Carthage, Tunisia

or early seventh century. The larger example was made of green marble with a moulded rim and was 1.54m across and 1.53m deep, much larger than the typical three-legged dining-table (*ibid.*, fig. 113; Ellis 2000, fig. 26). Tables with *stibadia* frequently show not only a central dish of food, but individual portions of food, usually bread, placed in front of each diner (Dunbabin 2003, pls 13-4, fig. 120). This suggests that these larger tables were used in a slightly different way from the typical dining-table, as a small dining-table of the type used with *triclinia* would not have been large enough to hold nine portions of food.

Masonry dining-tables

The dining-tables of masonry, summer or external *triclinia* were built as part of the structure, in contrast to the manoeuvrable tables required in internal dining-rooms, but the reasoning behind this is not clear. The use of water channels between table and couch and water jets in tables made stone tables suitable for some of the more elaborate *triclinia*, but most were much more basic. The tables were commonly cylinders of solid masonry, but square and rectangular tables are also known (see *20*; Dunbabin 1991, figs 8-12). The rectangular tables sometimes have a semi-circular indentation on the short edge of the table facing the front, perhaps for the addition of a portable table or a stand to hold a water-heater. The tabletops themselves were often made of decorative marble.

Table-cloths

Literary evidence

As the Latin word for table-cloth literally means 'hand-cloth' it is not always clear whether a table-cloth or napkin was meant. They are usually described as being made of linen, and would therefore be typically white as the Romans found linen difficult to dye deep colours. The biographer of Severus Alexander noted that his banquets were neither 'sumptuous nor yet frugal', and that 'none but snow-white cloths (*mantelia*) were used, and though they often had a scarlet stripe, they were never decorated with gold, though these had been introduced by Elagabalus, and even before his time, they say, by Hadrian' (*SHA*, 37.2). In this context, the reference could be to either table-cloths or napkins. Although covering up the dramatic wood grain of expensive tables would seem to defeat the point, Martial refers to a table-cloth used on a citrus table. While it might hide the expensive wood, it at least protected it: 'let shaggy linen cloth cover your citrus more nobly. On my round tables a circle [made by a wet glass] is acceptable' (*Epigrams*, 14.139). Ammianus Marcellinus refers to a linen table-cloth, decorated with a purple border to match couch-covers (16.8.8), and Sidonius to one of 'linen fairer than snow' (*Letters*, 9.13.33-4).

Artistic evidence

The three-legged dining-table is usually shown being used without a table-cloth. When they are used, the cloth is always short enough to leave the decorated bow of the leg visible. Examples can be seen on a table on a sarcophagus from Germany (Dietz *et al.* 1979, Abb. 122), and on a mosaic from Thyna, Tunisia (see *10*). The mosaic shows two tables, both of which have pinky-brown cloths decorated with black dots.

The folding table popular in Germany is always shown with a table-cloth that extends between a third and half-way down the leg. Some are shown with a fringe while others were made with a shaggy finish (see 25; Espérandieu 1965, no. 5146). Table-cloths, some shaggy and with fringes, were also frequently used on the low rectangular dining-tables.

The D-shaped tables used with *stibadia* are also sometimes shown as being covered with table-cloths, which usually reach the ground and hide the whole table. The Last Supper as depicted in the sixth-century Basilica of St Apollinare Nuovo in Ravenna takes place on a semi-circular couch with a D-shaped table set with pieces of bread and a large central dish holding two fish. The white, fringed table-cloth covers the whole table, and is decorated with a purple square and two L-shapes on the front face. Such long table-cloths appear to become more popular in the later period (Dunbabin 2003, figs 85, 107-8, 120).

SIDE–TABLES, SERVING– AND 'DISPLAY'–TABLES

The small size of the three-legged table(s) near the dining-couches meant that most of the food and drink had to be kept on separate tables and brought across by slaves whenever required. There is evidence for tables for the wine flagons and cups and for tables displaying silverware (presumably most hot food was brought in by course straight from the kitchen). Table types for use outside the dining-room include non-moveable stone tables placed in *atria*, peristyles and gardens, which, while they would originally have had a functional use, also became works of art designed to impress visitors. These often seemed to have been used for 'display' purposes, such as for the gifts and greenery laid out for the New Year celebrations.

The side-table (abacus)

Literary and artistic evidence

This was a table generally used to display vessels of silver or other precious materials. The rich could afford dinner services consisting of very large numbers of silver vessels, and any vessels not in use could be left on display during meals to reinforce the idea of their wealth. The Hildesheim treasure, for example, is made up of 70 silver vessels, including dishes set with busts in high relief that must have been purely decorative in function, while the 118 silver vessels found in the chests in the House of Menander in Pompeii were unlikely to have all been pressed into use at the same time.

In Cicero's speeches listing the crimes of Verres, he mentions how Verres had had made for himself enough gold cups 'to furnish half a dozen side-tables', and that he stole silver vessels from one Diocles Popilius, 'whose side-table [he] swept clean of all its vessels just as they stood there' (*Against Verres*, 2.4.25; 2.4.16). Sidonius wrote admiringly of the fifth-century King Theodoric, who dined in the Roman fashion, with couches covered in scarlet cloth or white linen, in a room where 'there is no unpolished conglomeration of discoloured old silver set by panting attendants on sagging tables' (*Letters*, 1.2).

The third triumphal procession of Pompey in 61 BC, when the spoils of war were paraded through Rome, included 'enough gold vessels inlaid with gems to fill nine side-tables' (Pliny, *Natural Histories,* 37.6.14), although he does not helpfully explain exactly how many vessels it takes to fill a table. A display of silverware on a table shown in the tomb of Vestorius Priscus, Pompeii, consists of 19 elegantly arranged pieces, including four graduated ladles in a row and two drinking horns on stands to keep them upright (*colour plate 13*). Underneath the table there is a large silver jug and handled dish of the type used for washing hands. The side-table itself is rectangular in shape, with stretchers placed about half way down the legs. The front of the table is decorated and the legs have elaborate capitals and feet, possibly of silver. The poor man, on the other hand, had little to display, so his side-table was more functional. Juvenal refers to one 'decorated' with six small water containers, probably of earthenware (*Satire* 3.204).

One-legged table

The one-legged table usually had a large rectangular top and a central leg which could either be column-like, bowed, or ornamented with sculpture. Examples made from stone are known, some of which were designed to rest against the wall of the room, and were clearly not a portable item of furniture. There are a number of possible functions for these tables.

Serving-table

The most common form of serving-table depicted on tombstones in Germany and France is a tall table with a single leg decorated with a lion's head towards the top. They appear to have been used mainly for holding containers for liquids rather than for food, in many ways fulfilling the role of a drinks bar. The clearest example that they were used as side-tables for meals comes from the Igel Monument, in a dining-room scene where two slaves are standing near one such table filling cups from flagons, while there are further flagons and cups crowded onto the table, with more on the floor underneath. A similar use can be seen on a sarcophagus from Cologne (Espérandieu 1965, no. 6492, surviving as drawing only) and a fragmentary relief from Neumagen (*ibid.*, no. 5154). Other images are more fragmentary, but all the tables are carrying containers for liquid (*29*).

One-legged side-tables were also used in the Mediterranean world, as is shown by the feasting scene now in the church of St Stefano, Pizzoli (*30*), where the table is freestanding and set between the two different groups of diners. It has a herm decorating the leg, and it holds drinks, and is tended by two slaves who carry the drinks to the diners. It is likely that the scene depicts a public feast, where those of a higher rank reclined to eat and those of a lower class sat up to eat; Dunbabin suggests the prominent position of the table in the relief could indicate that it had been given as part of the banquet gift (2003, 84).

These tables are noticeable for their height, being much taller than the dining-tables, and consistently shown as being chest-high to male slaves. Slaves were often depicted at a smaller scale when included in scenes depicting their masters (cf *18-9*), but the tables are shown as being tall even when no masters are included (*29*).

Display-table

Varro describes a *cartubulum* as 'a kind of stone table for vessels, an oblong rectangle with one pedestal. When I was a boy this used to be placed in many people's houses near the *impluvium*, and on and around it were placed bronze vessels' (*On the Latin Language*, 5.125). The use of the table for liquid containers is reminiscent of the side-tables, but this type of table was not in placed in the dining-room, but by the shallow water tank in the centre of the *atrium*.

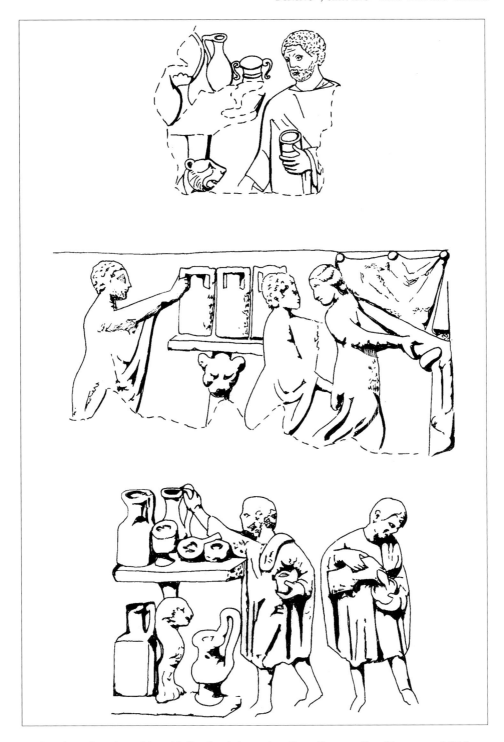

29 One-legged serving-tables with lion head decoration, from Germany. Top: Neumagen. Middle: Regensburg. Lower: Igel

30 Relief of diners at a public feast being served form a one-legged table. Stone relief, Armiternium, Italy. © *Deutsches Archäologisches Institut Rom (Neg. 84 VW 935)*

31 Circular tables with column legs, from Germany. Left: Abstatt. Right: Rottweil

The evidence from Pompeii suggests the table in this position could take a number of forms (see below), but as it was an item of furniture in a very obvious position, to be seen by any-one entering the house, these tables were often made of highly decorated marble as a work of art in themselves.

A table from Boscoreale, now in the Metropolitan Museum of Art, New York is a good example of a highly decorated one-legged table (Richter 1966, fig. 566). Its original position in the villa is unknown, but it could serve equally as a display piece in the *atrium*, or as a side-table in the dining-room to complement the decorated couches of the *triclinium* and expensive soft furnishings. It is made of marble and copper alloy, with a decorated bronze strip round the edge of the marble top and bronze feet on the bottom of the marble leg. The top is 1.06m long by 65cm wide, and has a height of 86cm (some 20cm taller than most dining-tables). Other one-legged tables from the Pompeii region have elaborate cast bronze legs including one decorated with a seated sphinx and one with a ship's rudder and a cupid riding a dolphin (Stefanelli 1990, cat. no. 25; Richter 1966, fig. 565). A stone table leg from Alesia, France, has full-length human figures, and it is likely the table leg in the form of a human figure shown in a mosaic showing the months of the year from El Djem is also made of stone (Solley 1979, fig. 5; Blanchard-Lemée *et al.* 1995, fig. 19k). The table is being used to display the ever-greens and gifts traditionally laid out at the New Year to ensure good fortune in the year ahead (Salzman 1990, 80, fn 75).

Stone table with possible ritual use

In Germany there was a fashion for circular stone tables with a single central leg. The leg was similar in design to a column, with base and capital, and could be decorated with mouldings and grooves (*31*). Surviving examples are usually associated with cellars, and it is has been suggested they were connected to a domestic cult (Carroll 2001, fig. 21). The overall height is usually in the range 90-125cm and the diameter of the top 70-110cm (Haug 1919), suggesting comparisons with the high serving-tables rather than the low dining-tables.

Stone tables, more usually rectangular, were also used for ritual purposes in the very late Roman period. From the sixth century, Christian altars often took the form of a tall one-legged table (Bidwell and Speak 1994, 103). As Christian rituals involved the serving of food and drink in imitation of the Last Supper, this type of altar probably developed from the serving-tables used during meals.

Stone side-tables

In Britain, fragments of at least 30 stone table-tops have been found. They are all concentrated in an area in the south-west of the country, and are usually found on villa or town sites dating to the late third or fourth centuries. As none have been found *in situ*, it is not know which type of room they were originally associated with, and therefore their exact use is unknown (Solley 1979). Two types have been identified; rectangular and a slightly larger version with a bowed front. Averages sizes are 92 x 61 x 8cm for the former and 135 x 82 x 13cm for the latter. They have square corner blocks and bevelled edges on the lower surface on three sides only, suggesting the fourth side rested against a wall as with a side-table, and may therefore have been used in dining-rooms. Both corner blocks

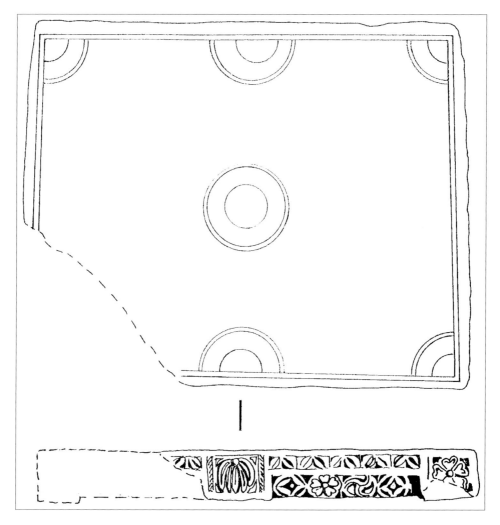

32 Decorated top from stone side-table. Rockbourne, Hampshire

and bevelled edge could be decorated with a form of 'chip carving', where deeply incised patterns form facets in patterns based on flowers, petals, triangles and other geometric forms. The top surface is usually plain other than a beading round the edge, but the example from West Park Villa, Hampshire, has compass drawn circles and sections of circles on it (*32*).

All the examples were found re-used and without legs associated with them, although a number of sites also produced short columns that Solley suggests could belong to the tables, as with the German examples. Other possible designs, known from elsewhere, include figures and bowed legs. It is suggested that the larger examples with bowed fronts may have had two legs (*ibid.*, 175).

33 Marble bench-table in the *atrium* of the House of the Wooden Partition, Herculaneum

Two-legged bench-table

This type of table had two solid legs like bench supports, and was designed to be seen from all sides. The evidence suggests that they were used particularly in houses with *atria*, where they were situated next to the water tank, perhaps as a display-table (*33*). Some examples have highly elaborate decoration on both sides of the legs, which is a type that appears to date only to the Augustan period (dell'Orto and Varone 1992, 263). The tables were usually made of marble, although it is suggested the top of the table found in the House of Cornelius Rufus in Pompeii was made of wood as only the legs survive *in situ.* The outer edges of both sides of the table supports have a curved, bowed profile, which can be wider than the table top itself. It usually takes the form of a winged creature with its head under the table top, the chest thrust forward to form the bow of the leg, with the body tapering down to a single claw foot. The animals can be lions, satyrs or griffins with wings that stretch back behind them on the flat face of the support. The space left between the wings can be filled by natural or stylised plant motifs, busts or cornucopiae (*34*). The decoration is found on both the outer and inner faces of the legs (Richter 1966, figs 573, 578-9). The table top can have a moulded edge, and occasionally projecting lion's heads, but is noticeably plain in comparison to the legs.

34 Decorated table support from Pompeii

An example found in the House of Meleager is made of a fine white marble and is 1.4m long, 80cm wide with supports 60cm high. The decoration consists of griffins with spread wings, with stylised plants surrounding a shield with a winged Cupid bust on the outer face, and a cornucopia with added bunches of grapes on the inner. It is suggested it was an import from the Hellenistic East (dell'Orto and Varone 1992, no. 183). Simpler versions, such as that from the House of the Wooden Partition have less decoration, restricted to the edge and outer borders of the legs (*33*). The foot can be carved into an animal paw, with foliage forming the rest of the decoration.

35 Stone table in the *atrium* of the House of M. Lucretius Fronto, Pompeii

Simple forms of the marble bench table could also be used in non-domestic settings. An example was used as a form of counter in a third-century shop in Ostia that specialised in selling fresh fish, It was free-standing near two entrances and close to a masonry counter. The legs were waisted, but have no decoration.

Four-legged stone table

Some tables placed in the *atrium* (and also the garden) were four-legged tables of marble, based on Greek originals. Most have legs of a rectangular cross-section, with claw feet and grooves on the outer face. There are decorated supports on the back of the legs that hold the rectangular table top (*35*).

Four-legged folding tables

The three-legged circular versions of the folding table were certainly used as dining-tables, as all the examples come from scenes of dining, with fruit on the

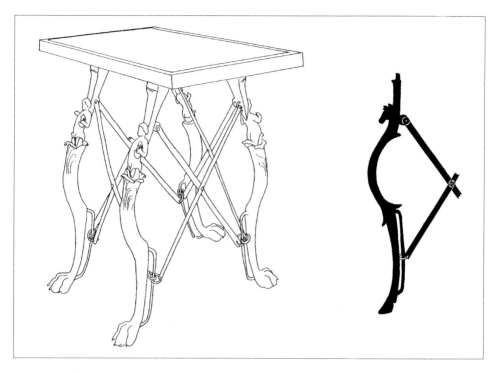

36 Bronze folding table with four legs. Left: Pompeii. Right: unknown provenance, Naples Museum

top and surrounded by men reclining on couches and women sitting in high-backed chairs. The function of the four-legged table is not so clear, as rectangular dining-tables are relatively rare. Folding tables may have been used to save space when not in use, or for travelling, although the example from Pompeii with a solid marble top was clearly not designed as a light-weight item (*36*).

The surviving examples from Pompeii have decorated bronze legs and a bronze-bound rectangular top of wood or marble. Each of the four legs are joined to one another by two metal strips that are hinged at the top and at the centre point where they cross, while the lower end has a ring attached to it that runs free on a metal rod and projects from the back of the leg. The tops of the legs have tenons that fit into holes on the underside of the table top, and it is only the positioning of the legs in these fixed points that locks the legs into a stable position. The legs have the same bowed effect as the three-legged Delphic tables, but being made out of bronze are more graceful. Above the bow one example has horse's heads and another a child emerging from leaves carrying a hare, and they have animal feet terminals like the wooden tables (*36*). The two tables from Pompeii have overall heights of 59 and 70cm, one a typical height for dining-tables, the other rather taller.

7

Desks and work-tables

DESK

Desks are depicted a number of times in scenes of every-day life on tombstones in the north-west provinces as well as in Italy. They are shown as large rectangular tables with solid sides and very short legs. The sides of the desk are frequently shown decorated with recessed panels, sometimes with a central roundel, but they can also be plain (*37*). The desk was not used in the same way as a modern desk. It had solid walls on all four sides (see *37*) and the man using it preferred to sit at one end.

Desks are shown used by landlords accepting rents and by people in shops, usually when writing or accounts is involved. In the scene from Neumagen, for example, the master sits at his desk on the typical high-backed chair, holding some over-large writing tablets, while bags of money rest upon the desk-top (*37*, top; cf Espérandieu 1965, nos 7725, 4037, 1341, 5243). A scene from Italy shows a man at a desk set up outside, apparently keeping track of the number of amphorae unloaded from a ship, while a soldier inspects some cloth laid out on a desk in a relief from Arlon (*37*, bottom).

TALL WORK–TABLE

Rectangular

Varro refers to a rectangular table called an urn-table (*urnarium*) 'because it was the piece of furniture in the kitchen on which by preference they put the urns filled with water'. Such tables were also found in bath-houses (*On the Latin Language*, 5.126). As piped water was not run into kitchens, and few houses had their own well or source of water, most Roman houses would have required

Left: 37 Stone reliefs of desks and chairs. Top: Neumagen, Germany. Middle: Igel Monument, Germany. Lower: Arlon, Belgium

Opposite: 38 Kitchen scene. Stone relief, from Igel Monument, Germany

somewhere to store water collected from external water sources such as wells or fountains. In small houses or apartments without separate kitchens, the jugs of water would have been kept in the main room, as suggested by Juvenal's description of the possession of the poor man Codrus, which included a side-table holding six small water pots (*Satires*, 3.203-7).

The best depiction of a table in a kitchen comes from the Igel Monument, where slaves are shown working in the kitchen. A man cuts up food standing at a sturdy rectangular table that is approximately waist height. The table has low stretchers and strengtheners at the angles, and is decorated with grooves (*38*).

Square

Tall square tables, simply smaller versions of the rectangular tables, are sometimes shown used in kitchens and shops. On the Igel Monument one is shown used for the washing up (*38*).

TRESTLE TABLE

Apparently more common as a general work-table than the four-legged table described above was the trestle table, which had the advantage of being both portable and capable of being stored away when not required. The rectangular top was supported on two trestles, each of which was an A frame, sometimes with a rectangular block at the top on which the table-top rested. A mosaic from Spain showing implements to be found in a kitchen includes two such tables, one laid out with joints of meat and a cleaver, and one holding a flagon and cups, which could be meant for wine but might equally be for the collected drinking water (see *73*). A trestle table being used to cut up meat is also shown in a kitchen scene from a sarcophagus from Rome (Dosi and Schnell 1986, 42).

Trestle tables were also used by market-traders and shop-owners to display their wares. Reliefs from Ostia show a table with lines of loaves set out for sale, one with dishes possibly holding some sort of grain, and another set with vegetables with a large crate stowed below (39, lower; Dosi and Schnell 1986, 39, 53). The tables were also used by craftsmen, such as the man laying out pieces for a floor or wall decoration made up of interconnecting pieces marble shapes of different colours (*opus sectile*) shown in a scene from Rome (*39*, top).

LOW TABLES

Rectangular
Low rectangular tables are used as general all-purpose tables. In the Simpelveld sarcophagus one holds three large glass bottles, and a musician uses one in a dining-room for the after meal entertainment (*colour plate 11*; see *21*). They were also used in bath-houses for holding bathing equipment or prizes for athletes (*40*; also Blanchard-Lemée e*t al.* 1996, fig. 135, from the baths at Thynia, Tunisia, where one is used to hold wreaths for wrestlers). All of them show a frame around the table-top, sometimes slightly raised above the rest of the top.

Square
Nothing but their function separates these from four-legged stools (see Chapter 8). A feast scene from a mosaic from El Djem shows slaves serving drinks from a large pitcher and two small jugs, the last two resting on a low square table (Blanchard-Lemée e*t al.* 1996, fig. 155).

Work-bench
The most common type of work-table was a long, low rectangular table, either with trestle legs or four corner legs. The height of the tables meant that the workers seated on stools could not get their legs under the table, and are often shown having to lean forward to work. Standing workers, such as the bakers preparing the dough on the tomb of Vergilius Eurysaces, work with bent legs and backs to reach the low tables (Kleiner 1992, fig. 93; Toynbee 1971, fig. 34). A wall painting from Pompeii shows wool carders seated behind low tables with fancy turned legs joined by stretchers on the short sides only (Kraus 1975, fig. 200).

   Some craftsmen also used the low table as a work-bench. Work-benches with trestle A-frame legs are shown on a glass bowl depicting carpenters at work, with soldiers using them for sawing, shaping and drilling wood (*41*). Some of the soldiers stand up to work, and two sit on four-legged stool, but all work from one of the short ends of the table. A wall painting from Pompeii showing Daedalus and Pasiphae, although probably based on a Hellenistic original, shows a similar table with highly splayed legs, with the piece of wood being worked

39 Trestle tables. Top: *opus sectile* worker. Incised marble panel, Rome. Lower: vegetable seller. Stone relief, Ostia, Italy

40 Low table. Mosaic, Baths of Porta Marina, Ostia

held in place by a series of pegs set in the table-top. The top from a small table or narrow stool from Castleford Fort is made of a piece of ash 60 x 30cm with four holes drilled at an angle so that the (non-surviving) legs would be splayed for stability (*42*).

Gaming boards

Men playing board or dice games sometimes laid a board on top of a table (the board usually larger than the tabletop), but could also balance the flat board on their knees as they sat facing each other sitting on chairs or stools. Such boards are shown on mosaics from North Africa and Greece, and on stone reliefs from Germany and France, and were presumably widespread throughout the Empire

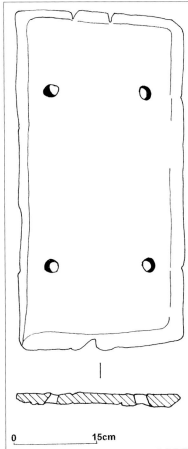

Above left: 41 Military carpenters using work-benches. Detail, gilt glass, Vatican Museum

Above right: 42 Wooden table or stool top from Castleford, Yorkshire

(Kraus 1975, fig. 224; Blanchard-Lemée *et al.* 1995, fig. 46). It is a method of playing games that required a surprising amount of trust, since the board could easily be knocked.

GARDEN FURNITURE

Over-sized marble versions of the three-legged dining table have been found at Pompeii and Herculaneum. A feline head is the most frequently used form of decoration on the leg, while the dog, so common on wooden examples, is never found (Mols 1999, 46). The fact that the marble examples have stretchers (unnecessary in stonework) suggests that they are copies of the wooden versions rather than vice versa. As they are not manoeuvrable they were not intended as dining-tables, and although they are found in gardens, they are never associated with external *triclinia*. Bench-tables and other tables made of stone are also found in gardens. It is likely most of these tables were not intended for a specific purpose, and were probably more artistic 'status' items rather than functional furniture.

1 Citrus-wood

2 Citrus-wood burr

3 Maple wood

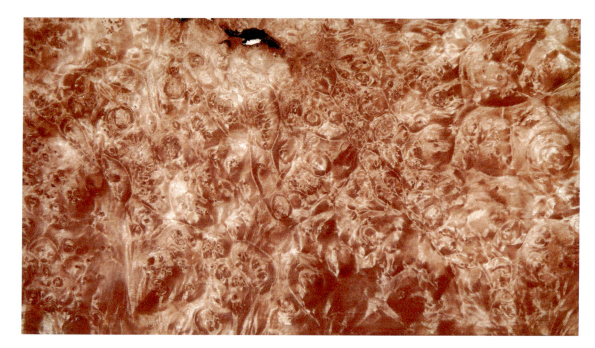

4 Maple burr

5 Walnut burr

6 A reconstruction of the wood mosaic from the stool from Herculaneum, in maple

7 Tortoiseshell

8 Reconstructions of bone appliqués as used on funerary couches and other furniture, decorated with red, blue and black wax. The back-ground is beech wood

9 Scenes from the life of Joseph in Egypt from the *Vienna Genesis*. © *Austrian National Library, picture archives, Vienna: Cod. Theol. Gr. 31, fol. 31*

10 The couch and wicker chair from the Simpelveld sarcophagus, Holland. © *Rijksmuseum van Oudheden*

11 The chest, low table, dining-table and cupboard from the Simpelveld sarcophagus, Holland. © *Rijksmuseum van Oudheden*

12 The external *triclinium* in the Garden of the Fugitives, Pompeii

13 Display of silver service set out on table. Tomb of Vestorius Priscus, Pompeii

14 Replica of a folding stool in use. © *Arbeia Roman Fort (Tyne and Wear Museums)*

15 Replica of a folding stool, folded. © *Arbeia Roman Fort (Tyne and Wear Museums)*

16 Scene showing couple on couch and chair. Wall painting, Ostia, Italy. © Archivio
Fotografico della Soprintendenza per i beni archeologici di Ostia

17 Tavern scene showing people drinking with food hung on a rack overhead. Wall
painting, Pompeii

18 Tavern scene showing men playing a board game. Wall painting, Pompeii

19 Tombstone of Regina, showing her sitting in a wicker chair and opening a box. © *Arbeia Roman Fort (Tyne and Wear Museums)*

20 Cloth, possibly used as curtain, from Egypt. © *The Textile Museum, Washington, D. C.*

21 Reconstruction of patterned cloth from Egypt

22 Reconstruction of patterned cloth from Dura-Europos, Syria

23 Reconstruction of desk and painted book cupboards. © *Arbeia Roman Fort (Tyne and Wear Museums)*

24 Reconstruction of a chest and a box. © *Arbeia Roman Fort (Tyne and Wear Museums)*

Stools and benches

The stool was the most common form of seating in the Roman world. One elevated form was used as a seat of state by high officials, but simpler versions were used equally by Emperors and slaves alike. They were to be found in taverns, in farmhouses, in workshops, in military camps, in bath-houses and in bedrooms. The design and quality of workmanship necessarily varied greatly and examples could be made from wood, bronze, or iron. Most were undecorated, but the more expensive versions could have cast or carved decoration, wooden mosaic decoration, carved ivory panels or coverings of silver or gold leaf.

FOLDING STOOLS

Curule seat (sella curulis)

This was a ceremonial seat of office reserved for magistrates (see Wanscher 1980 for a full discussion). It was restricted to use by officials such as consuls, praetors, city prefects, curule aediles, proconsuls, consular tribunes, censors, decemvirs, quattovirs, duovirs, some priests, Vestal Virgins and the Emperor. The word *curulis* came originally from *currus*, meaning chariot, implying that the seat was originally a seat used in chariots. The Romans believed it had been inherited from the Etruscans as a symbol of kingship, along with the *fasces* (symbolic bundles of rods originally used to punish wrongdoers), the leaf crown, the ivory sceptre with eagle, and the *toga praetexta* (a toga edged in purple, worn by magistrates and young boys). The seat had originally been used by the Roman kings, but from the early Republic its use was transferred to magistrates, and it continued to be used as such for the next 800 years.

The seat needed to be portable so that it could be carried by attendants to wherever it was needed, such as being placed on the tribunal in the Forum for the inauguration of the consuls on 1 January. A curule aedile ordered his to be brought to the house of a friend when some young men did not show him the respect due to him, so that he could flaunt his status in front of them (Livy, *Histories*, 9.46.8). The senior consul sat on one in the Senate house, which was an honour extended to Julius Caesar when he became Dictator (Wanscher 1980, 130). The seat was intended to be used only for business, although Julius Caesar was allowed to use it for any occasion as a special honour (*ibid.*, 1980, 130). The importance of the seat was such that when Consul Servilius Isauricus tried to stop Marcus Caelius carrying out any of his duties as a praetor he broke up Caelius' *sella curulis* to show he no longer had any authority (Dio Cassius, *Histories*, 42.23.3-9). Empty seats were sometimes set out for dead people, and were frequently used as a motif on Republican coins and on later tombstones (*43*).

The seat took the form of a stool with curved legs (either S-shaped or with inverted lion's legs), a highly decorated seat rail at the front and a thick cushion on top (Wanscher 1980, 149, 159). The rail at front and back were wider than the legs so that the ends would be visible when the stool was being sat on, as otherwise one of the most important distinguishing features of the *sella curulis* would have been invisible when in use. Images of empty seats often reflect this extra wide rail by having a tripartite decoration, with a wide central sector and a narrow band at either end (*43*, nos 1-3).

A probable example of a *sella curulis* was recovered during the early excavations at Herculaneum. The heavy folding legs were made of bronze with traces of gilding, and were cast in the shape of birds' heads with long beaks acting as the feet (*44*, left). Nearby, surviving only as an impression in the ash, was a decorated rectangle (showing a tripartite division) that was taken to be the organic seat rail (*43*, no. 4). The *sella curulis* is sometimes called the 'ivory seat', and it may be that the rail was typically made from it.

The importance of the decorated rail can be seen from the way it is emphasized in art. A folding stool is instantly recognisable when seen from the side due to the characteristic X of the crossed legs, but the side of the stool, being the part that folded, did not have a rigid rail suitable for decoration. On the coins depicting a *sella curulis* this results in the perspective being skewed so that the legs are shown from the side while the seat itself is shown from the front (*43*, nos 1-2). On tombstones the artists preferred to show the seats from the front. On a first century tombstone for Marcus Paccio Orino, for example, the front rail is shown in detail, with only the top part of the front legs and the lower part of the back legs being depicted, as the other parts of the legs are assumed to have 'disappeared' into the surface of the stone (*43*, no. 3). This shows the drawbacks of the frontal view, as it is not instantly recognizable as a folding stool, but the presence of the decorated rail was obviously of more importance than the legs

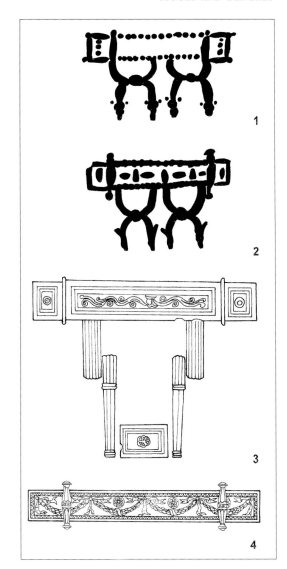

Right: 43 The *sella curulis.* 1–2: from obverse and reverse of a *denarius* of 59BC. 3: stone relief, Modena, Pompeii. 4: impression of organic seat rail, Herculaneum (*after Wanscher 1980*)

Below: 44 Bronze legs from *sellae curulis,* Herculaneum (*after Stefanelli 1990*)

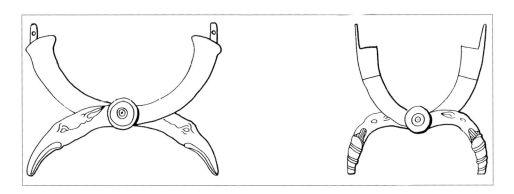

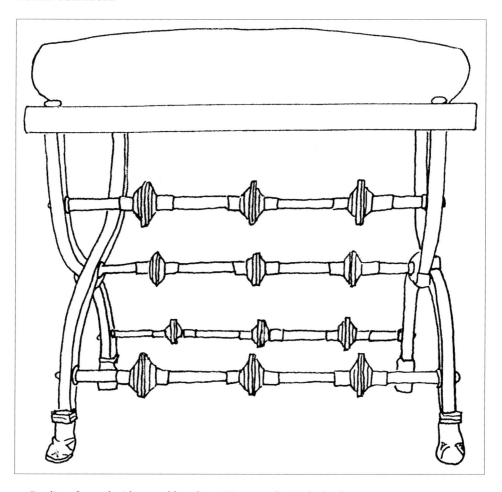

45 Replica of a stool with curved legs from Nijmegen, the Netherlands

(and the convention would no doubt have been fully understood by the Romans viewing the monuments).

It is unclear if the curved leg was used only for the *sella curulis*, but it seems likely, as the legs would make it distinctive when seen from the side, and the decorated rail when seen from the front. A faded painting in the tomb of Vestorius Priscus at Pompeii, depicting him sitting on a stool placed on a podium with crowds of people around him, takes care to show the curved bronze legs of the stool. The scene probably shows him carrying out his duties as aedile, a position identified in the inscription (Cooley and Cooley 2004, G88). A couple of images show women sitting on a stool with curved legs, but as at least one of these was an Empress, they may be women of rank given use of the seat as a special honour (Wanscher 1980, 324).

If curved legs were only for seats of honour, then a stool now in Nijmegen, Netherlands may be a *sella curulis*. It has curved iron legs connected by five irons, each decorated with three bronze discs, and has bronze terminals in the shape of human sandalled feet. No rail survives, so the whole seat section must have been made of an organic material (*45*). Rods with similar discs found at Newstead may come from a similar stool (Liversidge 1955, figs 39-41).

Gold seat (sella aurea)

Some 20 years after Julius Caesar had first earned the right to the *sella curulis*, and soon after he became Dictator, he was allowed to use his seat in the Senate house alongside the Senior Consul and was given the right to use the *sella curulis* on any occasion other than at the games. Soon afterwards, apparently as the next step up in the graduations of seats of honour, he was granted the use of a gold seat (*sella aurea*) to be used in the Senate (Wanscher 1980, 132-6). This was probably similar in design to the *sella curulis*, but distinguished by being gilded or decorated with gold fittings. He was sitting on this seat when he was assassinated, although Dio Cassius records that an attendant had originally removed it (clearly temporarily), thinking it would not be needed that day (44.17.3).

Double seat (bisellium)

The double seat, to be used at public shows, was sometimes given to officials as a mark of honour. It is found in the first century, but may not have been a long-lived type. Two officials at Pompeii were proud enough of the honour to have the seat depicted on their tombs (*46*). Both have elaborate legs with volutes or peltae-shaped elements and a flat front. The best parallels for which come from 'thrones', based on Greek originals, that are shown used only by deities in Roman art (Richter 1966, figs 482-3; 487-9). Both also have a fringed cushion long enough to hang over the two sides, and a plain footstool underneath. The inscription on the Quietus tombstones reads: 'To Gaius Calventius Quietus, an *Augustalis* [priest]. Because of his generosity, the honour of a double seat was given him by decree of the town councillors and by agreement of the people' (trans. Cooley and Cooley 2004, G37).

Folding stool with straight legs

This folding stool consisted of two rectangular frames pivoting on a central bar. The tops of the two frames were joined by leather or stout cloth that formed the seat, either as a sheet or as a number of straps to hold a cushion. Although the seat is often shown as being flat and not sagging below the frame it is possible a wooden board was sometimes also placed across the top of the frame. When sitting on a modern folding stool the bars of the frame are on either side of the

46 Double seat (*bisellium*) from tombstone of Quietus, Pompeii

body, while Roman stools had the top bar at front and back. Although this would appear to be more uncomfortable as the front bar would cut into the underside of the thigh, in practise this is not very noticeable, especially when a cushion is used.

Iron

Archaeological evidence

At least five iron-framed folding stools have survived from the Roman period. All of them share the same design where the upper bar at the front of the stool has been made in two parts, as in the examples found in burials at Holborough and Bartlow Hills (*47*). As this considerably weakens the strength of the frame, the two short sections of bars are supported by brackets, often S-shaped in design. These brackets, and the decorative terminals in bronze, create a pleasing decorative effect, but the brackets cannot be seen when some-one sits on the stool, and were not even very visible when the stool was set up but not in use. In fact, the brackets could be seen best only when the stool was folded up (*colour plates 14* and *15*). Three examples from Hungary show a further refinement, with

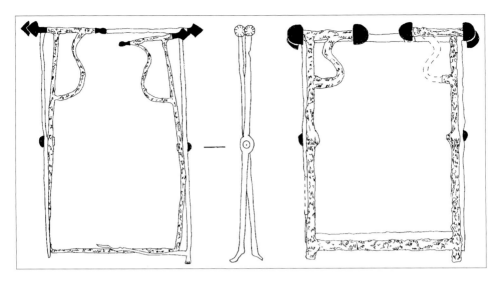

47 Iron folding stools. Left: Holborough, Kent. Middle and right: Bartlow Hills, Essex

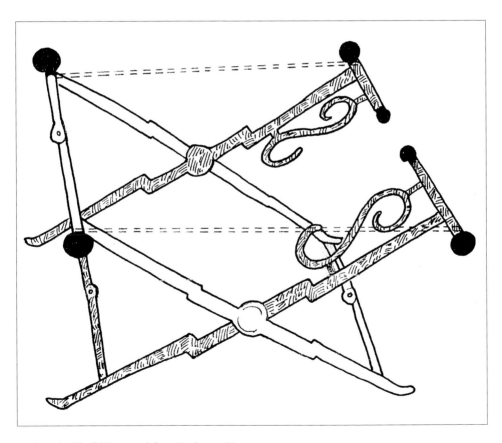

48 Iron double folding stool from Budapest, Hungary

hinges in the centre of the other three horizontal bars so that the stool could be folded in half again to take up an even smaller space (*48*).

The reason for the use of brackets on the front bar is unclear, as it is an elaboration that weakens the otherwise simple design. Although it is not visible when the stool is in use, it is just possible it had some status significance. The stool from Holborough, for example, had been buried within its own section in the burial mound, apparently after having been burnt on the funeral pyre, which suggests it had some importance (Jessup 1954, fig. 9). However, other examples found in graves seem associated with domestic items. The example from Budapest was found in a late third-century soldier's grave, including personal items and an axe, as well as a lamp, a silver spoon, a bronze vessel and a bronze jug, while at Bartlow Hills the stool was found buried with two strigils and a jug and *patera* dish used for washing.

Artistic evidence
A scene of a painter at work in the *Vienna Dioscurides* (very early sixth century) shows the painter sitting on a stool with a grey (presumably iron) frame and a red seat, shown dipping under the weight of the man (Weitzmann 1977, pl. 17). The scene of the temptation of Joseph in the sixth-century *Vienna Genesis* shows two women busy spinning, both seated on grey folding stools with red seats (*colour plate 9*).

Other metals
An elaborate folding stool from Ostia was made of silver–plated iron, with the whole frame covered in bead and reel decoration, solid silver ram's head terminals on the upper bars and silver feet in the shape of ram's hooves. Each of the upper bars (with no break in the front bar) had four figure-of-eight attachment loops to fasten the organic seat or the webbing that supported it (Wanscher 1980, 142).

Wooden
It is likely all-wood examples were also made, but it is difficult to be certain of the material depicted in stone sculpture. Possible examples include a representation of a furniture-maker working at a trestle table and a father grieving for his child (Liversidge 1955, figs 17, 64). The folding stools used as a camp stool by the military may also have often been of wood, as a lighter material to transport than iron (the reconstruction based on the Holborough original shown in *colour plates 14-15*, for example, weighs 13kg/29lb). The folding stool was associated enough with the military for the Emperor to be shown seated on this form of stool in images of him addressing his troops, rather than on the *sella curulis* to which he was entitled, in order to demonstrate his comradeship with the soldiers.

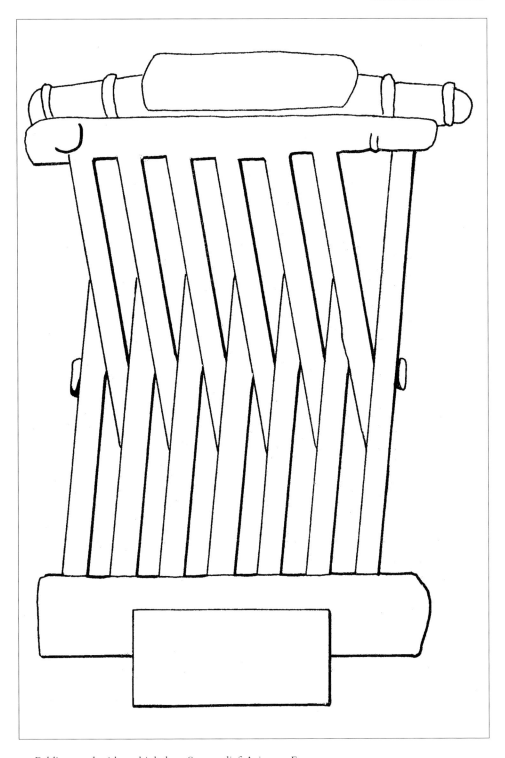

49 Folding stool with multiple legs. Stone relief, Avignon, France.

Folding stool with multiple legs

A few provincial depictions are known of stools with straight, multiple legs, numbering up to eleven per frame (*49*). The design was used by the Greeks, but is found in the Roman world only on stone sculpture in France and on some coins from Cyrenaica, and was apparently not otherwise widely used (Wanscher 1980, 131, 163). A tombstone for a *quattovir* from France shows a chair with seven legs per side standing empty flanked by *fasces*, suggesting it is a provincial version of the *sella curulis*, but there is no explanation why the chair should be so totally different, lacking both the curved legs and the decorated rail that identified the *sella curulis* elsewhere. t may be that arther than being a sella curulis, it is some other form of honorific seat. There is also a free-standing statue of a woman sitting on this type of chair (Espérandieu 1965, no. 2893).

NON–FOLDING STOOLS

Four-legged

This is the most typical Roman stool, with a square seat and four straight legs usually connected by stretchers. Most were probably made from wood, but some may have had metal legs and/or stretchers. Two men playing a board game in a wall-painting from Pompeii, for example, are shown sitting on stools with very fine, spindly legs which must have been metal (Kraus 1975, fig. 222). The legs are usually shown as being square in cross-section. This form of stool is used by people from all levels of society and in a variety of situations. It was used by workmen sitting by their work-benches (see *41*), by a rich woman watching her baby have its first bath (Huskinson 1996, pl.3, no. 2), and by men playing board games (Espérandieu 1965, no 7725). An example survives from Herculaneum, which is approximately 46cm square and 44cm tall, with the legs connected by stretchers both top and bottom (Mols 1999, cat. no. 23). There is moulding round the edge of the seat which is itself decorated by an elaborate star-shaped wood mosaic veneer (*colour plate. 6*).

Stools without stretchers may have had slightly splayed plain legs or more elaborately decorated legs, such as the one used by a woman watching her child being bathed, which has close-set spheres (Espérandieu 1965, no 5156; Huskinson 1996, pl. 3, no. 1).

Bronze

A small number of solid bronze stools are known from a number of first-century Italian sites, including Pompeii. They are square, with square-sectioned legs, and have a dished top similar to those on some benches. They can have openwork decoration just below the seat and on the stretchers placed about half-way down the legs. The decoration tends to be more elaborate on two opposite sides of the stool (usually that with the curved top edge) with simpler, or no decoration on the other two faces (dell'Orto and Varone 1992, nos 56-7; Ward-Perkins and Claridge 1976, no. 147). Their average height is just under 30cm, which contrasts with the typical height of wooden or stone stools and benches at Herculaneum and Pompeii that lies in the region of 36-45cm. It has been suggested they are foot-stools, in which case their height makes them suitable for use with beds rather than seats (see below).

Three-legged

Three-legged stools are the best type for providing a firm seat on an uneven floor, but they do not often appear in art despite the number of stools of the four-legged variety that are shown. They were probably more common in rural or poor houses, as suggested by Sidonius when writing about a friend who had just become a priest and was living in a suitably austere manner. As well as no longer having a down-filled mattress and a purple table-cloth, he had to get used to a three-legged stool as his seat (*Letters*, to Turnus 4.24).

Solid-sided

A potter working at his wheel in a wall painting from a shop in Pompeii sits on a stool with solid bench legs, and featureless solid square blocks are also sometimes shown in sculpture, although details of construction may have been intended to be added in paint. In France, there are a couple of examples of stools that appear to have solid sides and very short legs, reminiscent of the way some high-backed wicker chairs are shown (Espérandieu 1965, nos 4097, 5518). One of these has two diagonal bands forming a raised cross over the side of the stool, which is a motif also repeated on stools used by cherubs making garlands on a sarcophagus from Trier. The stools are probably made from wicker, but may be no more than baskets turned upside down, as they are very similar in design to one of the baskets used to hold the flowers used in the garland-making (Espérandieu 1965, no. 4989).

Cushions

Most folding stools, from *sella curulis* to camp stool, are shown with cushions, sometimes with a fringed cloth over or under it for extra elaboration. A mosaic from Piazza Armerina showing a scene in a bath-house depicts a man sitting on an iron folding stool with a very large, fringed cushion (*50*). The pattern on it suggests it is made from leopard skin. Elsewhere red cushions were popular (*colour plate 9*). Cushions are sometimes shown used on non-folding four-legged stools when

50 Man using folding stool. Mosaic, Piazza Armerina, Sicily

used in domestic settings, but are not as common in work-shop situations. Non-folding stools with decorated legs usually have a very thick cushion, set on top of a fringed cloth covering the top of the stool.

FOOT–STOOLS

The Roman foot-stool was typically a low, simple wooden stool presumably primarily used to keep the feet off cold, uncarpeted floors, although there is some evidence that they were sometimes a symbol of status. There is no evidence that cushions were ever used with them.

Foot-stools for stools

Small, often box-like footstools are often shown with the *sella curulis* (*43*; see also *46* and *49*). When depicted in sculpture, they are usually shown as being completely undecorated, in contrast to the highly decorated stools (Wanscher

1980, 161a, 167a; decorated, 165). The fact that they have still been included in the art implies some relevance to their presence.

Foot-stools for other forms of stools are not common, but are not unknown, and may perhaps be simply an indication of status since the stool itself was used by all levels of society. The scene from the sixth-century *Vienna Genesis* illustrating the temptation of Joseph shows a rich woman wearing a semi-transparent tunic (similar to that worn by the Pharaoh's wife in an earlier scene) sitting on an iron folding stool with a wooden foot-stool, while her more demurely dressed companion on a similar stool has none (*colour plate 9*). Foot-stools could also be used with four-legged non-folding stools, as shown in a relief of two people playing a board game balanced on their two laps, where the men share the same foot-stool (Rieche 1984, Abb. 40).

Foot-stools for chairs

Low wooden foot-stools are more often shown used in conjunction with chairs. They were generally square or rectangular in shape, sometimes box-like with solid sides, occasionally with four short legs, but most frequently with two bench-type legs with a curved leading edge to the front. A foot-stool was not apparently used with wickerwork chairs when the chairs were used for dining, but one is sometimes shown when the chair was used for other activities, such as hairdressing, reading and writing (55-6). A school master uses one with his wickerwork chair, although in this case it appears to be built into the chair. A foot-stool is occasionally shown used with straight-backed wooden chairs, such as in an ivory depiction of Herod watching children be killed (Weitzmann 1977, no. 406) and in a fragmentary scene from Neumagen (Espérandieu 1965, no. 5156).

In the school scene only the teacher out of the three seated figures has a foot-stool, probably as a mark of status. In mosaics from the sixth-century Basilica of St Apollinare Nuovo in Ravenna, the High Priests and Pontus Pilate use footstools, as do Jesus and the Virgin Mary when sitting on their jewelled thrones. The design of these thrones may be fantasy, but it suggests that at least in the sixth-century a footstool was an expected element of a seat of an important person.

Foot-stools for beds and couches

Varro refers to a stool for getting into a bed as a *scabellum* and one for getting into a higher bed as a *scamnum*, although this word also seems to have been used of benches (Cato, *On Farming*, 11.3: 'long stools'). These foot-stools have the same designs as those used with chairs, but are often much wider, and are most commonly shown in bedroom scenes, with sandals resting on them (*12*; cf

Liversidge 1955, pl. 17). They are generally absent from scenes showing couches used for dining, but this may purely be a matter of artistic convention rather than reality; the fresco from Ostia of a woman on a couch with a dining-table nearby does include a foot-stool (with sandals) under the couch (*colour plate 16*). Although Varro's statement suggests they were used as a step to reach the bed, they probably more often functioned like the foot-stools used with seats; as diners as well as sleepers took off their shoes to recline, a wooden foot-stool kept bare feet off cold floors until the shoes could be put on.

BENCHES

Varro explained the origins of the word for bench (*subsellium*) as meaning 'not a seat' (*sella*) (*On the Latin Language*, 5.128), but although the bench appears as nothing more than an elongated stool for two or more users, it had its own repertoire of designs that indicates a separate evolution. Some examples were designed to be free-standing, but many have decoration on one face only and were designed for use against a wall. They were used in peasant houses, farms, town houses and bath-houses, and were also the seats of senators and judges. They were used in particular in situations where there were large numbers of people to be seated, such as theatres, amphitheatres, odeons, and auctions (Suetonius, *Caligula,* 38; *Claudius,* 41).

Wood
Three wooden examples, of a size suitable for two or three people, have survived at Herculaneum. Two have two legs, plain at the back and with a decorative S-shaped front (*51*). The third has four legs, the back legs also plain and the front with the S-shaped profile. One example has a slightly dished seat decorated with incised lines and a spiral volute carved onto the side of at least one of the supports.

Bronze
The warm room of the Forum Baths at Pompeii contain three bronze benches approximately 1.5m (5ft) long placed round a very large brazier. All three have the same design, with a slightly dished seat and four bowed legs with cow-heads at the top and cloven feet terminals (*52*). The decoration is a pun on the name of the donor of the group of furniture, whose last name meant 'little cow'. The benches are inscribed 'Marcus Nigidius Vaccula, at his own expense'. The cost of all-bronze benches no doubt made them rare, but as with couches, there may have been some wooden benches with legs covered in bronze sheeting. A tavern

51 Reconstruction of a bench from Herculaneum. © *Arbeia Roman Fort (Tyne and Wear Museums)*

52 Bronze benches and large brazier. Forum Baths, Pompeii

scene from Pompeii shows at least one bench, and probably two, with bell-shaped elements decorating the legs (*colour plate 17*).

Marble

The bath-houses at Pompeii and Herculaneum also contain marble benches, some designed to be freestanding and some structural. In the woman's hot room of the Baths of Maschilius, Herculaneum, there are two free-standing marble benches. One has two legs, with a curved profile both front and back decorated with a floral design terminating with a pair of human feet (*53*). A longer bench against the opposite wall is of a different design in a darker marble and has the two legs set about a third of the way down the seat rather than close to the ends. These benches, although heavy, could in theory be moved. Elsewhere, fixed benches are found, such as the two benches in the Suburban Baths at Herculaneum which share three legs. These are broad, solid legs, flat at the back and curved at the front which is decorated with a number of vertical grooves (Pirozzi 2003, 75).

Other stone

In Britain there are a number of stone bench uprights which could have been used either with stone seats as with the all-marble benches from Italy, or else with warmer wooden seats. The supports have a flat back and decorative curved front, and were intended for use against walls. At the bath-house next to Chesters Fort on Hadrian's Wall, an example was found that had been left in position when the floor level was changed, suggesting a built-in bench the full width of the changing room. Another, with a similar flat back and curved front was found in the changing room of the baths associated with the fort at Mumrills, on the Antonine Wall.

Benches used in other buildings include one in a workshop in what was probably an official residence at Pentre Farm, Flint. The lower half, decorated with fluting and a stylised animal foot terminal, was found set 2cm below the floor alongside one wall. A more unusual L-shaped bench leg was found on a road surface inside Wallsend Fort on Hadrian's Wall, where the horizontal section for holding the seat is only 0.22m wide (*54*). Presumably the seat proper extended the full depth of the support, but was cut to accommodate the upright that may have acted as a divider or support.

Masonry

Where a large number of seats were required, such as in the changing-rooms in large baths, solid masonry benches were often built the whole length of two or more walls, sometimes finished with a covering of hard-wearing waterproof

53 Marble bench in the Baths of Maschilius, Herculaneum

54 Stone bench supports from Mumrills (*after MacDonald 1929*), Pentre Farm (*after Webster 1989*) and Wallsend

crushed brick mortar (*opus signinum;* see 67). Short masonry benches are sometimes also found outside the front doors of houses in Pompeii.

L(m)	H(m)	W(m)	material	type	reference
1.50	0.45	0.45	stone	free	Baths of Maschilius, Herculaneum
1.40	0.37	0.27	wood	free	Herculaneum: Mols 1999, cat. 24
1.05	0.39	0.33	wood	free	Herculaneum: Mols 1999, cat. 25
1.04	0.39	0.42	wood	free	Herculaneum: Mols 1999, cat. 26
–	0.48	0.32	stone	support	Petrie Farm: Webster 1989, fig. 32, no. 4
–	0.46	0.38	stone	support	Mumrills fort: MacDonald and Curle 1929, pl.36, b
–	0.44	0.32	stone	tomb	anonymous tomb, Porta Nola, Pompeii
–	0.38	0.44	stone	support	Wallsend: unpublished (maximum width only)
–	0.39	0.38	stone	tomb	Aesquilia Polla tomb, Pompeii

Table 2: Dimensions of free-standing and fixed benches

Cushions

A peasant couple cover a bench with a rough cloth in honour of guests (Ovid, *Metamorphoses* 8.639-40), while in a play by Plautus, Antipho's daughters bring him cushions to make him comfortable when he rests on a bench (*Stichus* 1.2). The bronze benches in the warm room of the Forum Baths in Pompeii, placed near a very large brazier, must have had some form of covering to prevent people using them being burnt by the hot metal. In this case, cushions seem more likely than a draped cloth to avoid hiding the expensive metalwork and decoration of the benches.

SETTLE

This term is used for bench-like seats with an integral back. These are comparatively rare, as there was a tendency for benches to be built or placed against a wall which could act as the back rest. A special type of seat-tomb at Pompeii, only granted to public benefactors by the town council, took the form of a semi-circular settle in stone. The type has a solid base, seat and back, often made of short sections of stone set together. There were usually large blocks acting as terminals at either end, which were as tall as the settle back, with a P-shaped profile decorated with scales, tendrils or feathers and ending in an animal-foot (Cooley and Cooley 2004, E40, G4-5; similar terminal stones are also used at the ends of some rows in theatres). Roman tombs were usually next to major roads, and such seats provided a service for weary travellers. Diners at a public banquet sit on settles drawn up to rectangular dining-tables and some drinkers in a tavern may have a similar seat behind their table in a scene from a sarcophagus from Ostia (see *28* and *74*). A clearer example of a settle is shown in a wall painting of a felt-maker's shop from Pompeii (see *75*). It has a plain upright back, as tall as the person sitting on it, and four legs with drum- and oval-shaped elements. All the examples are likely to have been made of wood.

9

Chairs

The most common forms of Roman seating, the stool and the bench, did not offer any back support. Chairs with backs, although they could be used by men, seem to have been considered more suitable for the 'weaker' members of society, such as women and the elderly.

THRONE

The Emperor was usually shown using the same type of seats as his subjects, such as the *sella curulis* and the camp stool. This was because a throne was an attribute of royalty, and the Emperors were usually careful to distinguish themselves from kings. In Roman art thrones were usually reserved for deities. In the early period a type with elaborate legs, tall back and sometimes with arm-rests, was copied from Greek originals (Richter 1966, pls 484, 487-8), and in the late Roman period Jesus and Mary are shown on thrones of a simpler form but decorated with gold, pearls and gems, and set with a thick red cushion (Bustacchini undated,122-3).

HIGH–BACKED CHAIR (*CATHEDRA*)

The most common form of Roman chair was a wickerwork chair with a straight front and a semi-circular back. The tall back curved round the seat, reducing in height to form arm-rests at the sides. This was a form of chair that was typically associated with women. A comment by Sidonius when entering a friend's villa shows men and women provided with different types of seating as well as reading material: 'the books near the matrons' chairs (*cathedras*) were

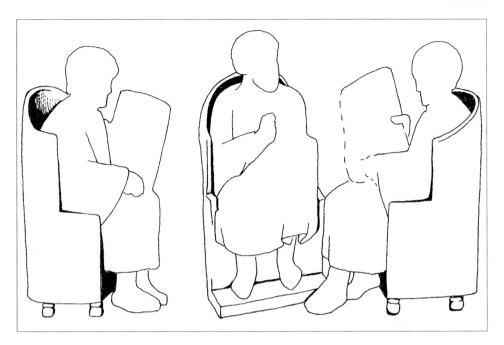

55 Teacher and pupils using wicker chairs. Stone relief, Neumagen, Germany

of a devotional type, while those among the benches of the father of the family were works distinguished by the grandeur of Latin eloquence' (*Letters*, 2.9 to Donidius), and in art most images show the wicker chair being used by women. Men shown sitting in one tend to be teachers, authors and philosophers. A relief from Neumagen shows a teacher and pupils sitting in this type of chair (55), and St Mark uses one while writing his gospel in an illustration in the sixth-century *Rossano Gospels* (Weitzman 1977, pl. 33). It was used by other men on special occasions, such as when the younger Pliny arranged a speech-reading, gathering his friends together in his dining-room 'and settling them on chairs in front of the couches' (*Letters*, 8.21.2). Comfortable chairs were a necessity in this case as the reading lasted two days.

The chair had a rounded back that was usually as high as the sitter's neck or shoulders, although an example from Koenigshoffen, France, shows a back as tall as the top of the sitter's head (Espérandieu 1965, no. 5518). The back could curve round to form the sides of the chair, or the sides could be cut back to form horizontal arm rests. The base is always shown with solid sides, although some examples have very short wooden legs.

The chair could come in a number of different colours. Pliny refers to white willow shoots with their bark removed and worked smooth as being suitable for making luxurious chairs (*Natural Histories*, 16.68.174). The late fourth- or early

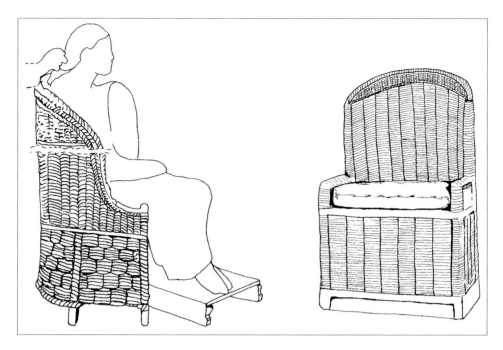

56 Wicker chairs. Left: stone relief, Neumagen, Germany. Right: stone sculpture in the round, Köln–Weiden

fifth-century mosaic showing the estate of the Lord Julius in the Bardo Museum shows a chair in shades of brown (Blanchard-Lemée *et al.* 1996, figs 120-1; note that the wife has the chair while her husband has only a simple stool), while the sixth-century *Rossano Gospels* shows this type of chair with the main body in white and the leading edge round the front a pale pink (Weitzmann 1977, pls 30, 33). The scene in the same manuscript showing Judas returning the silver to the high priest shows Annas sitting in a chair with a woven check pattern while St Mark sits in a chair with a horizontal herring-bone (*ibid.*, pls 30, 33). A number of patterns are used for the weaving, and it is possible different coloured wicker was used for further decorative effects. The wicker design of the lower half of the chair, up to the level of the seat, is often different to the design of the back and arms (*56*). Some representations in stone do not show the intricate detail of the woven wickerwork, and while it is possible these are a version of the chair made out of wood, it is more likely that the details of the wicker were added in paint (*55*). Most chairs, however simply carved, that show a back with a curved upper edge are likely to represent this type of chair.

In Britain, the wicker chair is depicted on tombstones of women such as Regina at South Shields (*colour plate 19*), the lady with a fan at Carlisle, and the daughter of Julia Velva from York (Allason-Jones 1989, figs 42, 5). Small pipe-clay

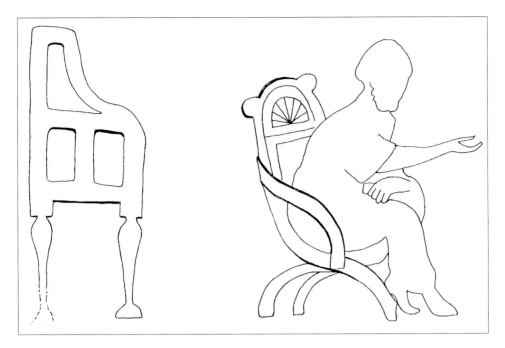

57 Chairs. Left: stone relief, Csákvár, Hungary. Right: manuscript illumination, *Vienna Genesis*

figurines, made in France but imported into Britain in some number, also show nursing mothers sitting in this type of chair (*ibid.,* fig. 51). Women also often used this chair for dining while their men-folk reclined (see *25*).

Cushion

The chair is always shown with a seat cushion, but never with one for the back. The cushions are shown clearly on two imitation wicker chairs made of stone found in an underground burial chamber at Köln-Weiden (*56*, right). A reference in the laws of the *Digest* (33.5) mentions the 'thick decorated coverings (*tapete*) with which chairs (*subsellia cathedraria*) are habitually covered'. No such covering can be identified from artistic depictions, unless it refers to the cushions covering the seats.

Straight-backed chair

Straight legs

In the north-west provinces straight-backed chairs similar to a modern dining chair are shown used by men in association with desks. They are made of wood, sometimes decorated with grooves, with a high back and legs joined by

58 Doctor sitting in front of a cupboard displaying medical equipment on the top and scrolls on a shelf inside. Sarcophagus relief, Ostia

stretchers or with a base with panelled sides. Some are shown with arm-rests (see *37*); those shown on the Igel Monument are made in the shape of a dolphin, which appears to be the only animal used to decorate chairs and beds. A seat cushion was sometimes used. In contrast, in Pannonia there was a local fashion for tombstones to show women sitting in straight-backed chairs. These seem a little more substantial, do not have stretchers and at least one has decorative turned legs (57, left).

Curved legs

A doctor shown on a fourth-century sarcophagus sits in a chair with curved legs like a *sella curulis*, but with a tall, upright back attached (58). The seat is unusual in that along the side of the seat and following the edge of the arm are a series of dots joined by shallow lines suggestive of upholstery and the attachment of cloth or leather to the wooden frame of the chair. There is no evidence that this type of upholstery was used in the Roman period, and it is probable that this simply represents some form of decoration on the wood. Another chair with curved legs is shown in the sixth-century *Vienna Genesis* (57, right). It has curved legs, curved arm-rests and a semi-circular zone of decoration on the back behind the user's head.

Folding chair

Some late Roman images appear to show women using a form of folding chair, although details of the chair are sometimes hidden behind the seated figure. On the fourth-century Proiecta Casket from Rome, the mistress applying her make-up is shown sitting in one such chair, which has two crossed legs on either side, with a decorated roundel on the pivot and another where the inner leg meets the seat. The same design can also be seen on an early fifth-century mosaic from a bath-house at Sidi Ghrib, Tunisia, which also shows a woman at her toilette (59). The chair is a pale grey colour, presumably either silver or iron, and has animal foot terminals to the legs. Behind the woman is the flat, upright back of the chair, the top of which is joined to the front of the seat by a chain. Similarly, the chair on the Proiecta Casket has a fancy chain and decoration on the top and sides of the chair-back. Both chairs have seat cushions, shown as a vague orange colour on the mosaic.

A third-century mosaic of three men playing dice from El Djem, Tunisia possibly shows a simpler design of this chair. It has crossed, slightly curved, thin legs with a tall, vertical back, and a dark line that may either represent arms to the chair or the connecting chain (Blanchard-Lemée 1995, fig. 46).

Birthing-chair

Roman women usually gave birth sitting up. A relief from Ostia shows the woman sitting in a chair that may have been a specially designed birthing-chair (Jackson 1988, fig. 24). In his book *Gynecology*, Soranus includes a birthing-chair when listing equipment needed for a birth that he expected the mid-wife to provide. The passage is one of the very few detailed descriptions of furniture from the

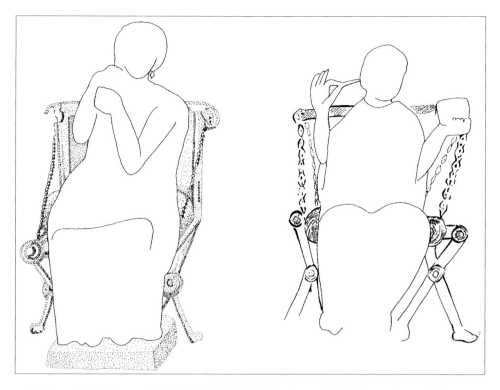

59 Folding chairs. Left: mosaic, Sidi Ghrib, Tunisia. Right: silver relief, Proiecta casket, British Museum

Roman world. 'In the middle of the stool and in the part where [the midwives] give support one must have cut out a crescent-shaped cavity of medium size…. And the entire width of the whole stool must be sufficient to accommodate relatively fleshy women too; and its height medium, for in women of small size a footstool placed beneath makes up the deficiency. Concerning the area below the seat, the sides should be completely closed in with boards, whereas the front and the rear should be open for use in midwifery…. Concerning the area above, on the sides there should be two parts shaped like the letter ϖ for the crossbar on which to press the hands in straining. And behind there should be a back, so that both the loins and hips may meet with resistance to any gradual slipping…. To the lower parts of the stool some people, however, affix a projecting axle which has windlasses on each side and a knob' for extracting a foetus that cannot be delivered alive (2.3[68]; trans. Temkin).

Other wooden chairs
The evidence of Roman art tends to suggests there was a range of chair designs which are represented by one or two examples, which may therefore reflect

regional or chronological differences. As they can differ noticeably in details of leg designs, arm-rests, height of the back and type of decoration, the impression is given that there was much more variety in chair design than in that of tables or couches. An example is that shown on a tombstone from Germany, where a woman sitting in a chair with a low curved back with individual bars connecting seat and arm-rest instead of a solid back, and long, splayed legs (see *25*, top; cf *57-8*).

10

Cupboards and shrines

CUPBOARDS

The free-standing wooden cupboard was developed by the Romans rather than being another item of furniture copied from the Greeks, and appears from the second century BC onwards. The evidence from Pompeii and Herculaneum suggests that within houses cupboards were used for objects in everyday use, such as eating and drinking utensils. The cupboards are found in dining-rooms, *atria*, bedrooms, kitchens and service-rooms, and only occasionally in store-rooms.

They appear in forms from alcoves and full-length recesses in walls furnished with shelves, through to small wall-mounted wooden cupboards, to free-standing cupboards ranging from those similar in size to modern bedside cabinets (50cm tall) to large units the size of modern wardrobes (over 2m tall). Most appear to be taller than they were wide, but an example more like a modern sideboard was found at Herculaneum, being wider than it was tall, although no traces of it now survive (Mols 1999, 57). The wooden cupboards often have sides and backs with characteristic long narrow vertical panels, doors with decorated square or rectangular panels and decorative mouldings round the top or base. A large cupboard from the *atrium* of the House of the Blacksmith, Pompeii (2.2m tall and 1.38m wide) had lattice in the door frames rather than panels (*60*, left). On the larger examples the doors tend to be as wide and as tall as the cupboard itself, but on smaller cupboards the doors frequently do not extend the full width of the front, and sometimes extend neither the full width nor the full height (*60-1*). Some doors do not appear to have any form of metal handle on the doors, others have small drop loop handles set near the edge of the door and a third group have wide straight drop handles positioned in the centre of the door (*60-1*; *colour plate 11*).

Above: 60 Wooden cupboards, shown to common scale to illustrate the range of sizes. Left: reconstruction based on a cast, Pompeii (*after Felletti Maj 1940*). Middle and right: reconstructions from Herculaneum (*after Mols 1999*)

Right: 61 Cobbler sitting in front of cupboard. Stone relief, Ostia, Italy

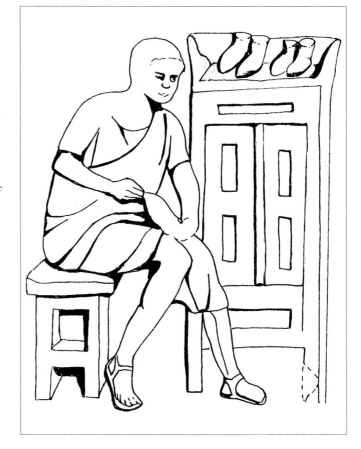

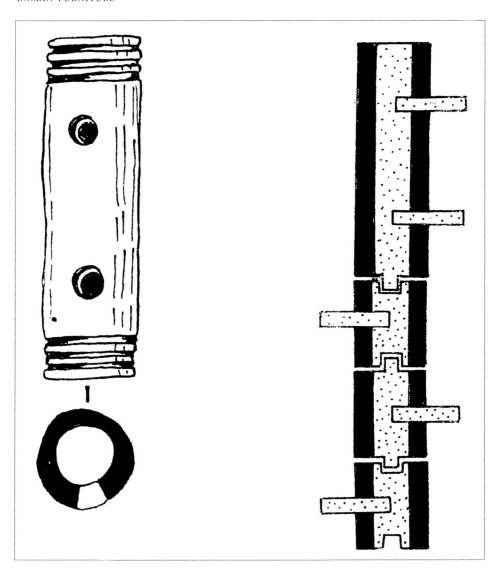

62 Bone hinges used on cupboards and chests. Left: typical two–hole form from Britain. Right: diagram showing how segments could fit together, with wooden core and pegs (stippled). Two- and one-hole segments shown

The doors were frequently hung using 'piano' hinges consisting of long bands made up of short cylinders fixed alternatively to door and frame by pegs. Those sections connected to the frame remained fixed while those connected to the door could move (62). The hinge sections were frequently made out of hollow bone, with a wooden core and wooden pegs. This type of hinge was considered decorative in its own right, with the bone hinges often decorated with incised lines filled with black wax, and there is evidence of the white bone hinges being used alternately with darker coloured woods (Mols 1999, 107-9; cf *66*).

Cupboards, like couches, were a prime item of furniture for decoration. A cupboard from a villa at Hayton in Yorkshire had delicate geometric designs inlaid in wood and bone (see *6*), while examples in and around Pompeii had diamond-shaped bone inlay, plaques with leaves and figures in relief, or appliqué mouldings and strips or inlay (Mols 1999, 106; fns 289, 676), and others again were painted (*colour plate. 16*; *63*: olive green and red).

Contents

Archaeological evidence

The contents of at least 20 cupboards are known from houses in or near Pompeii. The most common items found are consistently glassware and pottery vessels, followed by bronze vessels, lamps and dice. A cupboard in the dining-room of an apartment in the House with *Craticum* held dice, a string of glass beads, and glass and pottery wares on the top shelf, with more pottery on the middle shelf (Mols 1999, 130). Three cupboards found in different locations at the Villa of the Pisanella District, Boscoreale, contained not only the usual eating and drinking vessels but also some more exotic items, including two sets of surgical implements, toilet items with a silver mirror, and two swords (Mols 1999, 130). Four cupboards were found in the peristyle of House of Iulius Polybius in Pompeii, and four in the *atrium* of the House of the *Cryptoporticus*, which contained a mixture of items including a statuette, bronze- and silverware, a lamp, two bronze candelabra, a gold ear-ring, four lead weights and a balance (Mols 1999, 131). A cupboard in the *atrium* of the House of the Trojan Shrine was used to store at least some food, as a vessel containing fish bones was found inside it (Allison 2004, 127).

Literary evidence

In the early Roman period special cupboards were placed in the *atrium* to store the masks or busts of the ancestors, only to be opened to display the contents on special occasions, but it is not clear if this tradition out-lasted the *atrium* house, which had fallen out of favour by the end of the first century AD (Mols 1999, fn 317). Plautus implies food could be kept in cupboards (*Two Captives*, 4.4.10), although this never appears to be as common a content as household objects. Pliny mentions that an application of vinegar with either red poultry dung, the ash of a shrew-mouse's tail, earth from a swallow's nest, a swallow-chick reduced to ash or the skin of a snake pounded in wine with a male crab would kill moths 'when put away by itself in chests and cupboards' to protect clothes (*Natural*

63 A cupid working at a desk as a perfume-maker, in front of a cupboard. Wall painting from the House of the Vettii, Pompeii

Histories, 29.32.101). Expensive soft furnishings could also be kept in a cupboard (Cicero, *Against Verres*, 2.4.12).

Alcove cupboards

At the House of the Gems, Herculaneum, there was a cupboard created by making a rectangular recess in the wall of a service room (61cm wide, 47cm high and 22cm deep). It was plastered inside, like the rest of the room, and had a single wooden shelf rested on a slot cut in the plaster. It may possibly have been closed by wooden doors (Mols 1999, cat. no. 38), and contained bronze, glass and pottery vessels.

Wall cupboards

A small cupboard, with only the back-board now surviving, was found nailed to the wall of an upper bedroom in a house in Herculaneum (Mols 1999, cat. no. 35). The surviving piece is approximately 80cm tall and 60cm wide.

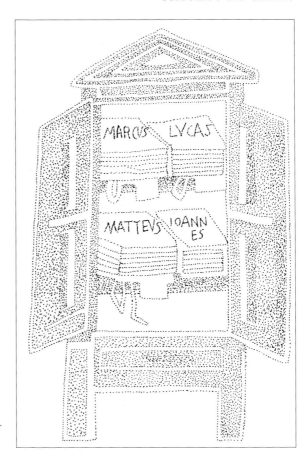

64 Book-case. Mosaic, Mausoleum of
Galla Placidia, Ravenna, Italy

Free-standing cupboards

Tall cupboards

With legs and gable top

The cupids acting as perfume-makers in frescoes from the House of the Vettii,
Pompeii, have a tall, narrow cupboard with four internal shelves (63). It has panelled
doors and a pediment with mouldings and some form of decoration within the
gable. The cupboard contains a large figurine of Venus on the top shelf and vessels
on the remaining shelves. As the scene involves cupids at work, the details may not
be fully accurate, but the cupboard is similar to other Roman cupboards (64).

With legs and flat top

Another scene of cupids at work, from the House of the Hinds at Herculaneum,
shows a different form of cupboard in their workshop. This is almost as wide as

it is tall, with a flat top and at least three internal shelves. The doors are panelled, with one small square panel at the top and a large rectangular panel below. Because of the width of the cupboard folding doors are used.

A second-century wall-painting from a tomb at Ostia shows a tall, thin cupboard with short legs, a deep base and two panelled doors (*colour plate 16*). The doors have spots on the four panels and on a central horizontal bar, with close-set dots down the batten that covers the join between the two doors when shut. The dots are black on the top two panels, red on the lower ones and alternate black and red on the central cross-bar. The use of two colours suggests that these do not represent metal studs (known to have been used on room doors) or the shadow of lattice inserts as used on the doors of the cupboard from Pompeii (see *60*, left). It is possible the dots are painted decoration on the cupboard. In the painting, the body of the cupboard is left white, in contrast to the red and black of the couch and chair, and has a black top and coloured motifs on the front and side of the base.

Medium height

With legs and flat top

A bas-relief of a cobbler at work from Ostia shows him sitting to one side of a cupboard set on short legs, with two panelled doors (see *61*). The doors have a batten to cover the join between them, but no means of opening them are shown. The top of the cupboard has low walls on three sides and has been used to display merchandise. The height of the cupboard is unclear as the artist was more concerned with fitting the scene into the space available, and the seated cobbler on one side of the cupboard is only slightly smaller than a standing cord-maker on the other side. However, as the top of the cupboard is being used for display, it is unlikely to have been too tall.

Another cupboard used for display is shown in a bas-relief on the sarcophagus of a doctor found near Ostia, where a case of medical implements has been propped on the top (*58*). This cupboard is more ornate than the cobblers', although it shares the short legs, flat top and panelled doors. This cupboard is shown with the doors open revealing two visible shelves and has two zones of decoration above the doors, possibility representing beading and wood-mosaic veneer, and there is a deep base below, the function of which is unclear. More modern parallels would suggest a drawer, which although rare, were used occasionally in Roman cupboards.

Without legs and flat top

A cupboard containing pottery vessels found in a kitchen at Herculaneum had two shelves, including the floor of the base (see *60*, middle). It was 1.3m tall, and approximately twice as high as it was wide, with two panelled doors. The space between the base and the lowest shelf also had an inner set of small panelled doors.

The second-century Simpelveld sarcophagus depicts a cupboard without feet and a flat top. Although the size of the cupboard is unclear as the furniture is not shown to scale, the proportions of the two doors and their handles suggest it is not large. It is slightly taller than it is wide, with two doors with elaborate mouldings on the four panels and a batten to cover the joint between the doors. Each door has an unusual straight horizontal handle rather than the more common loop handles (*colour plate 11*).

Small cupboards

With legs and flat top
An example from Herculaneum has comparatively tall legs and boards on three sides of the top like the cobbler's cupboard described above, so that although the whole unit is approximately 1m high, the actual cupboard space is only about 50cm tall (Mols 1999, cat. no. 39). It has an awkwardly small central door for entry into the middle section, limiting the uses of the storage space. It contained two pottery lamps, a jug and a dice, and was found with a bed in a first floor room.

Without legs and with flat top
Another small cupboard from Herculaneum, without legs or boards round the top is approximately 50cm tall. Above the cupboard space (accessed by two small, inset doors), there is a single drawer with a round bronze knob (see *60*, right). Two other cupboards with drawers, one apparently similar in size and the other larger, have been found at Pompeii and Herculaneum (*ibid.*, 57, 131). Drawers were generally not common in the Roman period, only occasionally being found in cupboards and then only as single examples. Nothing like a chest-of-drawers was known.

Book-cases and cupboards
Book-cases (for scrolls) were found in the library of the Villa of the Papyri in Herculaneum, described in a letter of 1754 as a room 'adorned with presses, inlaid with different sorts of wood, disposed in rows, at the top of which were cornices' (Mols 1999, 64), suggesting individual cases rather than shelves lining the walls. Pliny had a 'cupboard of the type used in libraries' fitted into the wall of one bedroom for books that deserved to be constantly reread (*Letters*, 2.17.8), and niches in a wall of house VI, 17, 41 in Pompeii were used to store scrolls (Mols 1999, 64).

Although it is not clear from the description if the free-standing cases in the Villa of the Papyri had doors, some book cupboards shown in art certainly did, such as the cupboard shown on the sarcophagus of the doctor which had scrolls on its shelves (see *58*). Cupboards with doors and pediment tops were also used as book-cases. A mosaic from the fifth-century Mausoleum of Galla Placidia, Ravenna, has such a case with two shelves on which codex books, in this case the four gospels, are on display. A similar cupboard is also shown in the Codex *Amiatinus*, produced in the eighth century but with images considered to be based on Byzantine originals (Weitzmann 1977, 126). The cupboard is painted red, with white decoration of animals and geometric patterns.

SHRINES (*AEDICULA*)

Household shrines could take the form of alcoves in walls, masonry structures, or purpose-built wooden cupboards shaped like temples. The shrine was an enclosed space designed to hold statuettes, busts and figurines of deities, as well as the offerings made to them. As the shrine was designed to hold numerous but small statuettes, it had to be positioned at a respectable height above ground-level by being built into a wall, raised on top of a solid masonry base or placed on top another item of furniture. At least one wooden shrine surviving at Herculaneum was built with a household cupboard below it, and in the *Satyricon* Petronius describes 'a large cupboard (*armarium*) in a corner [of the *atrium*], in which was a shrine with silver Lares, a marble statuette of Venus and a gold box' (satyricon, 29). Cupboards may also have been used as combined storage and shrine simply by using different shelves. The wall painting of Cupids making perfumes from the House of the Vettii shows a tall cupboard with glassware on the three lower shelves and a statuette of Venus on the top shelf (see *63*).

Alcove

Numerous examples of this type survive at Pompeii. Although the simplest form of shrine was just painted onto a wall, others were set in a recessed niche, the more elaborate examples having a projecting pediment and pilasters in the manner of miniature temples (de Franciscis 1978, pl.192; Stefani 2005, cat. no. 10).

Masonry

Sometimes an alcove was combined with an altar or a solid masonry base built in front or near it (*ibid.*, 28, 29, cat. no. 12). More sophisticated versions had a masonry shrine built on top of a base that stood proud of the wall. These frequently have an arched recess, and almost all have a pediment roof and columns or pilasters, and they could be highly decorated with stucco work and painted plaster (65; Stefani 2005, 28). The shrine in the *atrium* of the House of Red Walls, Pompeii, had a painting of a Genius and dancing Lares on the back wall, and the space between the columns (*c.*50cm wide) contained bronze figurines of two Lares, Aesculapius, Apollo, Hercules and Mercury, with a bronze lamp set in front of them (Boon 1983, 45).

Because of their position at a height above ground level, few survive elsewhere in the Empire, unless built into cellars. A rare example from Rezé, France has survived with its occupants. It was made of tiles set in concrete and was *c.*60cm wide and *c.*30cm deep and survived to a height of 32cm, although it had originally had an arched top. It had been covered completely in lightly marbled red stucco, including the small central recess which was *c.*30cm wide and 15cm deep. This held two pipe-clay figurines of standing female figures, with traces of gilding on their hair, which were placed on either side of a pipe-clay female bust. In front of the left-hand figurine was a pipe-clay figurine of a seated dog, and in front of them all was a yellow-painted stone statuette of a boar (*ibid.,* pl. VII).

Wooden

Wooden examples were also based on the shape of a temple, often with a pediment roof and columns at the front. Unlike masonry examples, these had folding doors to reveal the inner shrine itself. One example sat on top of a cupboard, which may have been to economize on space as it stood in a small room (Mols 1999, cat. no. 29; 66). The room, in the House of the Wooden Shrine, was a bedroom that was possibly also used for eating. There was an alcove for a bed, traces of which were found but not preserved, and a round table. Like all the surviving fragments of shrines from Herculaneum, it was well-made, and had fluted pillars with Corinthian capitals and a border of wood-mosaic round the top. It was found with a bronze statuette of Hercules and a marble statuette of a goddess, possibly Venus, in the shrine section, as well as some household items. The cupboard, with similar decoration to the shrine, contained household items such as glassware, jewellery and coins.

The other examples are more fragmentary. One comes from an apartment in an upper storey consisting of a living-room leading to a kitchen leading to a bedroom. The shrine was found in the badly lit bedroom, where the only light came through the rooms in front of it (Mols 1999, cat. no. 28). Another was found, apparently hanging on the wall, in a bedroom possibly also used as a living-room which contained a full-size bed and a child's bed as well as a wooden sculpture and a large number of bronze statuettes (Mols 1999, cat. no. 27). It may have contained statuettes of Jupiter, Aesculapius, Diana, Minerva, Harpocrates, two Fortunas and two Lares, as well as a weight, plate, coins and

Above: 65 Masonry shrines. Left: House of the Tragic Poet, Pompeii. Right: House of the Black Room, Herculaneum

Left: 66 A reconstructed shrine based on examples from Herculaneum. © *Arbeia Roman Fort (Tyne and Wear Museums)*

Opposite: 67 Masonry bench and shelves. Baths of Maschilius, Herculaneum

glass paste pieces (*ibid.*, 132). This had red-painted stucco surviving on some of the exterior surface, and white stucco over the interior. Pieces of a fourth example were found in both the peristyle and dining-room of the House of the Black Room, and may well have originally come from an upper room (*ibid.*, cat. 29). This had marble Corinthian capitals, with surviving traces of red paint, at the top of the fluted wooden columns. Most of these shrines were found in rooms that functioned as bedrooms, in contrast to the masonry shrines which are usually found in *atria*. Suetonius mentions bedroom shrines used by both Hadrian and Domitian (*Augustus, 7, Domitian, 17*).

SHELVES AND RACKS

Wall-mounted shelves
Single planks of wood set on a bracket or brackets have been found in a number of buildings in Pompeii and Herculaneum, perhaps the most famous being the one in Herculaneum torn from the wall leaving a cross-shaped scar originally taken to be evidence of Christianity (Mols 1999, figs 162-3). Short shelves, such as this example and one in the kitchen at Boscoreale have a single central bracket, the example at Boscoreale being made of iron and extending above

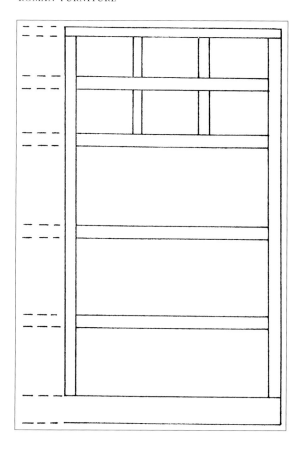

Left: 68 Free-standing wooden shelving, Herculaneum (*after Mols 1999*)

Below: 69 Suspended wooden *amphora* racks from Herculaneum (*after Mols 1999*)

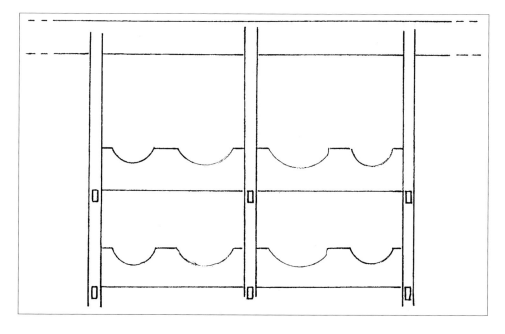

the level of the shelf (Jashemski 1987, fig. 16). A longer shelf with more brackets is shown in the wall painting of Cupids working as cobblers from the House of the Stags, Herculaneum (Naples Museum, inv. 9179). Long masonry shelves, covered in plaster and painted, and usually with upright dividers to form separate compartments, were used in bath-houses (*67*).

Sets of shelves

A shop in Herculaneum had a set of shelves that rested on the floor and fitted into the wall for stability. Perhaps half of the original structure now survives, as there is space beside it for the same again and broken timbers suggest the unit extended to this side (*68*). There are three full-width shelves and two shelves divided into three cubby-holes. Brooms were supposed to have been found on one of the shelves (Mols 1999, cat. no. 34). Smaller sets of shelves were used on tables (*39*), and the taverns at Pompeii often have sets of stepped masonry shelves built into one end of the masonry counter (Stefani 2005, 102).

Other shops in Herculaneum selling liquids had racks attached to the upper wall or suspended from the ceiling to hold *amphorae* (large pottery vessels used for transporting principally wine, olive oil and fish sauce). Surviving examples all have two shelves with boards at the front cut with semi-circular notches to keep the jars steady, and could hold eight, nine and 24 *amphorae* (*69*; Mols 1999, cat. nos 31–3).

Beams

Food could be suspended directly from pegs or hooks driven into roof beams and brought down when needed by using a forked stick. Suspended frames of wood set with pegs were also used. A mosaic from Marbella depicting kitchen implements has birds, fish, joints of meat and something green hanging up on such frames (see *73*). A scene of people drinking in a bar from Pompeii also shows food, including sausages, hanging from a beam suspended over the customers (*colour plate 17*). Beams were also used in fullers' work shops, where cloth or clothes could be draped over a suspended beam whilst they were being worked on.

11

Chests and boxes

The presence of over 50 chests and boxes from Pompeii and the surrounding towns and villas suggests they must have been one of the most common items of furniture in Roman houses (Mols 1999, 63, 134-7). They seem to have been used more frequently for storage than cupboards, possibly because cupboards were more sophisticated items of furniture which must have cost much more than simple chests. Chests also had the advantage of being relatively easy to transport. They seem to have been used for secure storage more often than cupboards as locks are more often associated with boxes than with cupboards; the very plain chest depicted on the Simpelveld sarcophagus, for example, is shown with a very visible keyhole (*colour plate 11*). Due to the weight of the contents the larger chests generally rested straight on the floor or on battens across the width of the base, although smaller boxes sometimes stood on short legs.

A surviving chest at Herculaneum had a piano hinge, such as was used for cupboard doors, but the segments were all made of wood rather than bone. Mols suggests that this was because the hinge was largely unseen at the back of the lid so more decorative bone versions were unnecessary (1999, 109). Elsewhere, iron strap hinges were common.

Strong-boxes

Wooden strong-boxes with locks for holding bags of money or other valuables were sometimes kept in the *atrium* of those houses possessing this formal space. Some *atria*, as a 'public' room, had display items of furniture such as elaborate marble tables designed to impress visitors, so a large, metal-bound money chest could also be used to demonstrate the wealth of the owner. Juvenal refers to the most common prayer heard in temples as being 'Let my wealth grow! Let my strong-box be the largest in the whole *forum*!' (*Satires*, 10.2). One possible strong-box, now in Naples Museum, has a base of wood but is almost entirely covered

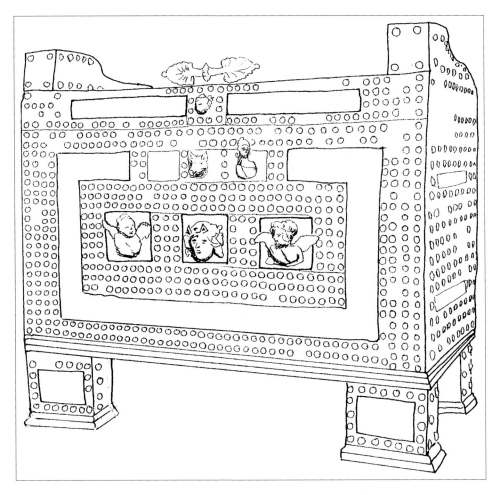

70 Strong box from Pompeii, decorated with bronze plates, studs and reliefs

in sheets of iron and bronze, including a large number of studs (*70*). The front alone has a palmette handle and 738 studs as well as projecting busts of Diana, three cupids, a boar and a lion. The presence of the busts show it was more than just a functional piece of furniture, and would have been an eye-catching item of furniture suitable for display in a public area.

Chests (arca)

Archaeological evidence
Chests were used for general storage of a wide range of goods, so their location in a house depended on their use. They were found in store-rooms, bedrooms, studies, *atria* and peristyles and other rooms not so easily identified, frequently

including those on upper floors. The House of Menander in Pompeii produced six chests in all, including two with bronze fittings and one with lock and fittings set against a wall in the peristyle, and two containing a silver service which was possibly crated up for transportation rather than in storage (Mols 1999, 63).

At the House of Argus in Herculaneum, four chests were found in a storeroom that was also provided with racks holding food in pottery vessels. One box contained food and glassware, one food, one flour and a smaller one ten coins. Another chest from the town contained flour and textiles (Mols 1999, 134; cat. no. 41). In Pompeii, a chest in the *atrium* of house I, 6 contained pottery and glassware; one in a study in I, 6, 4 contained a glass service and jewellery, and one in a bedroom in the House of Trebius Valens contained valuables including bronze vessels, silver spoons, and an agate unguent bottle. At Boscoreale, a chest contained clothes, glass bottles and bronze toilet articles (*ibid.,* 135, 137). The most varied contents came from a bedroom in the House of the Two *Atria*, where one chest was empty while a second contained two bronze vessels, a bronze bell, wax tablets, two pouches containing money, three spoons, glass, spices and grain and a small wooden box (*ibid.,* 136). Wax tablets (usually used for legal documents) have been found in chests in at least four different houses, often in bedrooms. That from the House of the Bicentenary held *c.*150 tablets in total.

L	W	D	
150	80		with bronze fittings
150	55		containing silver service
120	80		containing silver service
70	32	32	from peristyle
60	30		from room 43
35	24	21	from *oecus*

Table 3: The sizes of chests from the House of Menander, in centimetres

Literary evidence

The most common use for chests in the literary record is for storing clothes, and it is noticeable that there are many more references for clothes being stored in chests than in cupboards. Cato includes a clothes chest in his list of equipment for a farm and explains the use of *amurcum* (the lees of olive oil) to keep moths away: 'So that moths will not attack clothes. Boil *amurcum* down to half, and with it coat the bottom, the outside, the legs and the edges of the chest. Clothes may be stored in it once it has dried' (*On Farming* 11.3; 99) Putting citrus leaves, wormwood or malabathron in chests with the clothes would also discourage insects (Pliny, *Natural Histories*, 12.7.15; Dioscorides, *On Medical Matters,* 1.166, 3.26, 1.11). Martial refers to 'numerous' sets of dining-clothes, consisting of tunic and mantle, kept in a small chest (*Epigrams,* 2.46), while Columella refers to apples being stored in a type of small chest of beech and lime 'of the type used for storing business clothes but somewhat larger' (*On Farming*, 12.47.5). Chests were also used to store bed-clothes (Horace, *Satires,* 2.3.119).

*Press (*prela *and* pressorium*)*

The press was used to smooth clothes by using pressure. The only surviving image of one shows a large rectangular frame holding two long screws pressing a board down onto another, with layers, presumably of cloth, between them. It comes from a wall painting in a fuller's house in Pompeii and may represent the type of press used by a professional and not the type found in more domestic situations, where the press was also, according to literary evidence, used for storage. The descriptions refer to silks or clothes of shimmering colours in the presses, so it is possible they were used only for the more expensive items of clothing. Ammianus Marcellinus refers to enough clothing for eleven men 'shimmering with shifting light' in a press (28.4.19), while the Empress was also considered to store her silks on one (Martial, *Epigrams* 11.8; see also 2.46, for cloaks stored in one, and Claudian, *Epithalamium of Palladius and Celerina*, 101).

Packing cases

Shops in Pompeii and Herculaneum have produced crates or chests containing quantities of pottery lamps, glassware and samian ware, probably all still in their original packing cases (Mols 1999, 135).

Boxes

Small versions were often used for jewellery or other valuables, and were more frequently decorated than the larger chests. Two small chests were found with the skeletons of the people who had sheltered in the vaults on the beach at Herculaneum, containing jewellery, coins, a perfume bottle and copper alloy vessels. Smaller boxes, of the type found in graves, were probably used as jewellery boxes that sat on a table, but some were free-standing boxes with legs, such as that shown on the tombstone of Regina from South Shields (*colour plate 19*; cf *colour plate 24*). It sits besides her wicker chair, and has short legs with a stretcher across the front, metal fittings at the corners and a lock plate. She holds open the lid to reveal the contents which are no longer recognisable, but the presence of the lock suggests they were her valuables. The box is decorated with an appliqué of a crescent, of a type found at Intercisa, where the fittings from a number of

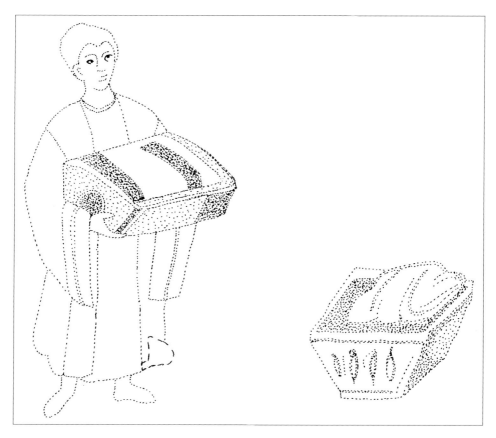

71 Open-topped-boxes. Left: slave carrying clothes to the baths. Mosaic, Piazza Armerina, Sicily.
Right: box from toilette scene. Mosaic, Sidi Ghrib, Tunisia

small boxes have been recovered. These include strips attached to the box with
decorative copper alloy studs, plates with repoussé decoration and drop-handles,
all of which are also common as loose site finds (Crummy 1983, figs 85, 90-1).
Boxes could also be decorated with bone appliqués, in the form of strips incised
with dot-and-ring or parallel lines that could be filled with coloured wax, strips
carved with variations of bead-and-reel, and plaques decorated with relief,
incised or painted figures (*colour plate 8*; St. Clair 2003, figs 3.11, 9-15).

Open-topped boxes for clothes

Clothes and probably towels were carried to bath-houses in open-topped boxes.
They helped to keep the clothes uncreased between storage and use as they were
carried from one part of the house to another, or even from one building to
another if the bath-house was built separately. It is possible that clothes were also
stored in these boxes in bedrooms, either by themselves or stacked into chests

or cupboards. An early fifth-century mosaic from the entrance to a bath-house at Sidi Ghrib, Tunisia, shows a seated woman surrounded by a selection of the items she would need for her toilette. The objects include a large silver wash bowl, a silver bucket, water jug and slippers as well as a rectangular box. Its colour suggested wooden construction, containing a crumpled white cloth which could possibly be a towel or discarded tunic. The box is relatively deep, and wider at the mouth than at the base (*71*, right).

A mosaic in the fourth-century villa at Piazza Armerina shows members of the family walking to the bath-house, accompanied by one slave carrying a perfume box and another carrying a folded white tunic with blue stripes in a large off-green rectangular box (*71*, left). Another mosaic in the bath-house showing a man being towelled down after his bath has a slave holding out a white tunic with red and black stripes on top of a mantle or cloak with L-shaped decoration. The clean clothes are still folded from storage and may have been carried to the bath-house from their chest or cupboard in a similar box (see *50*). The fourth-century silver Proiecta Casket from Rome has scenes of a procession to a bath-house and a woman at her toilette, and in both cases attendants hold boxes, some of which may well have been for clothes (Shelton 1981, pls 8-10).

12

Curtains and floor coverings

CURTAINS

Latin texts are sometimes translated in a way that could suggest the Romans used wall hangings in the manner of medieval tapestries. However, those who would have been rich enough to be able to afford the amounts of cloth necessary (always an expensive commodity in the ancient world) seem to have preferred to decorate their walls with marble veneers or elaborately painted schemes instead, although a display of silver from the tomb of Vestorius Priscus in Pompeii with a small cloth hanging behind it suggest it was not totally unknown on a smaller scale (*colour plate 13*). Such references may in fact be referring to the hanging draperies of window-curtains, door-curtains, or inter-column curtains.

The cost of the cloth came from the amount of work and materials required to dye the wool, hand-spin the thread and then weave the cloth on two-beam or warp-weighted looms. A fragment of a surviving account list from Vindolanda Roman Fort gives an idea of the first-century costs of complete curtains. They were the most expensive items in the list, with recorded prices of 54.5 *denarii* for one in scarlet, 46.5 *denarii* for one in green, over 44 *denarii* for two in purple and over 55 *denarii* for one in yellow (Birley 2002, 152).

Usually equal ratios of dye-stuff to material were required, so that the 'ordinary cover' weighing 10lb mentioned in the fourth-century Edict of Maximum Prices, costing 500 *denarii*, would have required 10lb of dye-stuff such as the root of the madder plant or lichen (29.7). One pound of wool dyed in 'fourth quality' archil purple cost 300 *denarii*; one pound of wool twice dyed (for a stronger colour) in 'best genuine purple from Miletus' cost 12,000 *denarii* (24.12; 24.6; trans. Graser 1975). After being dyed, the wool was spun into thread for weaving. A striped blanket or curtain from Dura-Europos, Syria, not even 1.5m square, required at least 8km (5 miles) of thread, and would have required even more if it had been

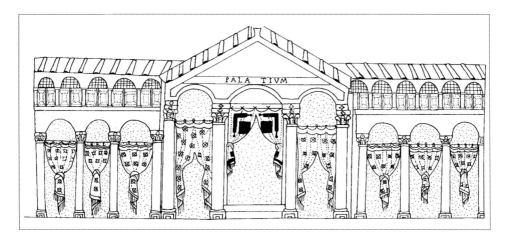

72 Curtains used between columns. Mosaic, Ravenna, Italy

set up on a warp-weighted loom. A weaver could get wages of between 15-40 *denarii* per pound of wool woven, according to the type of thread, while a linen weaver got between 20-40 *denarii* per day, plus maintenance (21). Those weaving elaborate patterns would have been paid more.

Curtains were hung on poles with a limited number of rings, creating a characteristic draped effect between them. Pliny mentioned the fruit of the *cucus* tree which had a hard kernel that was used to make curtain rings, and a large number of metal loops found in the Roman *agora* at Athens have been identified as curtain rings (Pliny, *Natural Histories,* 13.18.62, Richter 1966, fig. 600). The sixth-century mosaic of Theodoric's palace also appears to show one set of curtains attached by ties (*72*, central curtains).

Window curtains

Curtains were occasionally used over windows, but were probably more common in rooms such as bedrooms with large windows where it would be useful to be able to cut out light, rather than being routinely used on all windows. Wooden shutters were certainly used both over those with glass and within window openings without glass as an alternative way of cutting out light as well as keeping out wind and rain. When Pliny the Younger had inflamed eyes, he explained in a letter: 'I can darken my bedrooms by drawing the curtains without, however, making them too shadowed. The light in the *cryptoporticus* [lower level colonnade often half underground] can be just as dim when the lower windows are covered up', perhaps with wooden shutters as with an upper colonnade shown in a mosaic of Theodoric's palace, where there are glass panes in the upper part of the arches and wooden shutters in the lower half (*Letters,* 7.21.2; *72*).

Many windows probably had no form of covering. An illustration of Queen Dido in the early fifth-century *Vergilius Vaticanus* shows her in an expensive room with marble (either real or painted) on the walls and a coffered ceiling, but while there is a white door curtain there are no window curtains over the small four pane window placed high up near the ceiling (Weitzmann 1977, pl. 3). Many windows, like this example, would have been too high to be covered.

Door curtains

Curtains were sometimes used in internal doorways of rooms, including bedrooms, sun-rooms and dining-rooms. The curtain was left down when privacy was required, and hooked back to indicate when people could enter (*SHA Severus Alexander*, 4.3; Augustine, *Confessions*, 1.13; Seneca, *Letters*, 80.1). Such curtains had also proved useful to people in the unsettled times between the murder of one Emperor and the succession of another. After the murder of Caligula, Claudius 'hid himself amongst the drawn curtains' of a sun-room until a soldier spotted his feet, while Varius, the cousin of Severus Alexander 'hid himself in a corner and placed over himself the bedroom-curtain which was at the entrance to the bedroom' when he was frightened by the clatter of approaching soldiers (Suetonius, *Claudius* 10; *SHA Elagabalus,* 14.6).

Curtains were also used in exterior doorways. Juvenal describes decorated doors, hanging curtains and greenery on the threshold on the entrance of a bride's new home (*Satires,* 6.227), and Augustine refers to curtains at the entrance of schools hiding what was within (*Confessions,* 1.13). They are shown used at the entrance to the Temple in Jerusalem and in a doorway in the Governor's Palace in sixth-century mosaics at Ravenna in the Basilica of St Apollinare Nuovo (Bustacchini undated, 110, no. 3; 115, no. 4). These 'historical' images perhaps reflect the contemporary use of external curtains in important buildings, since churches and associated buildings certainly used them at this time. In 394, a church man travelling in Syria saw a dyed and painted curtain with an image of Christ or a saint hanging in the doorway of a church (Hartley *et al.* 2006, 191-2), and they are shown used in front of external doors on buildings belonging to the church of the Holy Sepulchre, Jerusalem (Cornell and Matthews 1982, 190).

When required the curtain could be held back by a hook or tie of some type, but at other times the curtain itself was tied in a knot, usually to one side of the doorway (such as the curtain held by a courtier in the mosaic of the Empress Theodora and her court in Ravenna; *ibid.*, 218-9).

Column curtains

The original purpose of hanging curtains on bars stretched between rows of columns was to provide extra shade within a verandah. That they were also used simply for decorative effect is suggested by examples shown tied in a central knot. The mosaic showing Theodoric's palace has a number of different styles of curtains between its columns (*72*). The curtains are white, with red, blue and gold decoration and long fringes, with more elaborate patterned tapestry-woven elements on the central pair of curtains. In the colonnades there are single curtains tied in a central knot and in the central range there are pairs of curtains, hooked or tied back against the columns to either side, with a pair of curtains tied in a knot against the two central pillars.

Canopies

Canopies, tied to the branches of convenient trees, were used by diners such as hunters having informal picnics outside (Dunbabin 2003, pl. 8, fig. 30), and they may well have been used over some external *triclinia* which did not have vines or nearby trees to provide shelter from the sun. A wall painting from Pompeii suggests canopies could also be used in verandahs used for dining (*ibid.*, fig. 29). Horace describes a disaster in the middle of a meal when 'the canopy spread above came down in mighty ruin upon the platter, trailing more black dust than the north wind raises on the Campanian plains' (*Satires,* 2.8.54), and although there is no reference to the meal being held out-of-doors, there seems no evidence to suggest canopies were used indoors. More references to the cost and quality of such canopies could be expected in literature, when other dining-room furnishings such as couch-covers and table-cloths are mentioned freely, if it had been a widespread fashion for use in internal rooms. The mosaic of Empress Theodora in Ravenna shows an apparent canopy with broad stripes of red white and blue, but it is unclear if it is supposed to be in or outside (Cornell and Matthews 1982, 218-9).

Archaeological evidence

A number of complete or near-complete cloths have survived from the Roman world that are curtains, blankets, couch-covers or other forms of drapery for furniture, although it is now impossible to identify their exact use. Literary evidence refers to cloths with pictures used as bedspreads and couch-covers, so figured textiles that might seem suitable for vertical curtains to modern eyes may have been used spread over couches (see Chapter 5 above; see also Lucretius, *On the Nature of Things,* 2.34-6).

The splendour of soft furnishings available to the rich can be seen in these surviving textiles. Many of them are tapestry woven, which involves undyed warp (vertical threads) with the pictures and patterns created by building up discreet blocks of colour one after the other in the weft (horizontal thread). The great majority of coloured work was done in wool, as, unlike linen, this could be dyed rich colours. They could be highly decorated with a riot of human figures, animals, and floral and geometric designs in many colours covering every inch of the cloth.

One of the largest examples is a fourth-century tapestry-woven cloth from Egypt, so skilfully woven there is no obvious front or reverse. It had perhaps been specifically designed to be seen from both sides, although its length would make it a very tall door or inter-column hanging (*colour plate 20*). The surviving fragment is 1.8m wide x 3.25m long, and has a series of 13 horizontal bands of decoration consisting of interlace and geometric patterns, some with birds and busts and edged with borders, flowers set in squares on a back-ground of dots, wreaths with fruit and birds and medallion busts, friezes of dogs and wild beasts set against foliage and cupids holding birds, wreaths and branches. The main colour of the cloth is red, but in total 19 different colours were used.

Stripes were a very popular form of decoration, whether plain or inhabited with geometric designs or images of humans or animals. Another cloth from Egypt has wide horizontal bands of red and yellow decorated with delicate geometric patterns in blue-green and navy blue. Fifteen different patterns, many of them repeated, are used (*colour plate 21*; Trilling 1982, cat. no. 108). Other examples include rows of birds between lines of foliage on a red background, broad green stripes with black decoration alternating with plain red bands, and red and black decoration forming stripes against a yellow background (Hartley *et al.* 2006, cats 169-71). A fragment from Dura-Europos in Syria, has geometric strips between thinner strips of graded colours and another has at least two rows of four-petalled flowers against a green ground (*colour plate 22*; Pfister and Bellinger 1945, frontispiece). A blanket or curtain from the same city, re-used as a shroud, has 65 vertical stripes in 11 colours (*ibid.*, pl. XVI).

Rarer examples of surviving curtains have an image designed to fit a specific size of cloth. One, 2.1m long x 1.1m wide, almost certainly from the same workshop as that shown in *colour plate 20* has a repetitive lattice section in the centre, consisting of a grid of stylised leafs in two shades of green, containing alternating birds and bunches of grapes. The pediment has a jewelled border, a central square containing four flowers and is flanked by birds and leaves. The columns themselves have elaborate capitals and bases, carefully shaded shafts, and decorative swags. Although at least eight different shades are used in total, the background colour is again red (Trilling 1982, no. 2). Another has a border on all four sides of winged horses between trees, while the central area has Nereids on dolphins and men in boats in a field of papyrus on a red background (Weitzmann 1979, cat. 150). Another fragment of textile, sadly incomplete, appears to have a more freehand design. The third-century curtain or covering from Egypt has a rich blue-green background with a variety of fishes swimming across it, with shadows beneath the fish creating a three dimensional image (Weitzmann 1979, cat. 182).

Other curtains had elaborate, but small, geometric shapes or bands woven into a plain background (see *72*, central curtains), but few of these curtains survive complete as the decorated sections were often cut away from the plain cloth to be sold separately on the antiquities market. In Egypt the main body of cloth on such curtains or furniture covers sometimes has extra loops in the weft to create a shaggy appearance like a modern towel, which is perhaps an example of a local fashion, although the shaggy table-cloths from the north-west provinces may have been made in the same way (*25 and 26*; Trilling 1982, cat. nos 14, 69, 84). Other furnishings were undecorated, and cannot now be distinguished from mantles or cloaks.

FLOOR COVERINGS

Roman floors ranged, according to wealth, from beaten-earth floors, flagstones, mortar floors (often containing crushed tile to provide a waterproof flooring), wooden boards, floors made up of marble slabs cut to form geometric patterns, and mosaics. Those with expensively patterned floors would have had no desire to cover them up. There are various examples of a simpler mosaic design being laid where it would mainly be hidden by permanent pieces of furniture, such as dining-couches, with the elaborate art restricted to the areas of the floor where it would be visible to guests (see *17*).

Lower down the social scale mats (*teges, matta*) were sometimes used, made out of rushes such as the *mariscus* rush and the inner bark of papyrus (Pliny, *Natural Histories,* 13.22.72; 16.70.178; 21.69.112). Martial mentions mats in reference to two poor men, both of whom were living in cheap housing. One, Nestor, is said not to posses even 'a patched mat of absorbent rushes', while a mat is listed amongst the few possessions of the other (Martial, *Epigrams* 11.32; 11.56). There are also references to the use of mats as bedding. An unfaithful wife conceived children 'on frame-beds and mats' belonging, amongst others, to a cook, a wrestling coach and a musician, who would either be slaves or members of the urban poor, and according to Juvenal the Empress Messalina preferred a mat in a brothel to her bed in the Palace (Martial, *Epigrams*, 6.39; Juvenal, *Satires*, 6. 118). In the fifth century Augustine mentions a sect of Christians called the 'Mattarians' because they slept on mats instead of beds (*Against Faustus the Manichean*, 5.5). It is not clear how wide-spread the use of mats was, although they would seem to be an attractive proposition on mortar or stone floors in mid-winter. There does not appear to be any evidence for cloth carpets or for strewn rushes.

13

Furniture in use: farms and the poor

Rural poor

Roman literature provides a number of word pictures of the houses of poor people, and although fictional portrayals cannot be taken as fully authentic representations they are of value in that they at least provide an idea of how a Roman thought a poor person's house should look. In Book Eight of *Metamorphoses*, Ovid tells the story of the gods Jupiter and Mercury visiting the homes of a thousand people. The only place where they are given a friendly welcome is in the house of a poor peasant couple called Philemon and Baucis, so in reward the couple are allowed to live while every-one else is drowned in a flood. The house was thatched with straw and marsh reed, and the couple lived in it alone without any slaves. They stored split wood and dry twigs within the roof space and hung smoked bacon from a roof beam. For furniture they had a bench large enough for two and a willow-wood couch with a mattress filled with sedge-grass that the guests reclined on for the meal. In honour of their guests, the bench was covered by a cloth and the couch by a cheap cloth 'they were not accustomed to bring out except on holidays'. They also had a three-legged table with one short leg propped up by a potsherd. They had a forked stick for lifting down the food hung on the roof beam, something to rake out the ashes from the fire (which may have been no more than a piece of wood), a small bronze vessel used to boil the meat for the meal, communal pottery vessels and baskets for serving the food, a pottery bowl for mixing the water and wine, and waxed beech-wood cups for drinking.

In a fragmentary section of the *Satyricon* (135-7) Petronius describes the cottage of a priestess called Oenothea in similar terms. He mentions copper, pottery, basketry and wooden vessels like those of Ovid's peasant couple, and a forked stick to lift down a bag containing both beans and a pig's cheek, and refers to dried herbs, raisins and serviceberries also hung up in the smoky rafters. A peg in the wall held a twig-broom and there was an open fire for cooking. For furniture there was a little table used for preparing food, a bed and a seat (sella) that collapsed when the woman stood on it to hang up the bag of food.

In the poem *Moretum*, reputedly written by Virgil, the farmer Simylus lives with a single slave, a woman called Scybale. The house has an open fire and food hanging from the ceiling, although instead of 'hams and slices of bacon dried and salted' there were only cheeses hung in baskets. There was a closet (an 'enclosed space') with a lock, used for storing grain, and a quern for grinding it to flour. There was a frame-bed, a smooth board (on a table?) used for mixing and kneading bread dough, and a small shelf designed for holding a lamp, but no other furniture is mentioned. There was a sieve for the flour, a mixing bowl and a brush made from a tail that was used to clean the quern.

The descriptions give a similar picture of rural cottages in the Mediterranean region consisting of a single room with an open fire, dual use bed/dining-couch, a table for food preparation rather than for dining, and food stored in the roof space where the smoke from the fire would help preserve and protect it from insects.

Urban poor

The poor living in tenements in large towns or cities were equally likely to be living in a single room, but the centre of the home was no longer the open fire, as the lack of chimneys in the multi-storey buildings made them impossible. Portable charcoal-burning braziers provided heat and the opportunity to cook, but they lacked some of the advantages of an open fire, such as the provision of light. As the urban poor were not self-sufficient in food, there was less need to store food in their homes, but there was probably more need to store water, depending on the proximity of the nearest public fountain and how many flights of steps needed to be climbed. In Rome Juvenal describes the room of a poor man called Codrus as possessing a bed that was too small for a dwarf, six small water-pots on a side-table with a small drinking cup and a marble statue below, and an old chest containing Greek books (*Satires*, 3.203-7). Martial describes the belongings of Vacerra and his family (wife, mother and sister) when he moves house as consisting of a frame-bed with three surviving legs, a broken table, a leaking chamber-pot, a lamp, a wooden bowl, an unpolished brazier, a water-pot full of salt fish and other food including a rope of onion and garlic, and a pot of turpentine (12.32).

Farms

The earliest surviving Latin work of prose is a book by Cato called *On Farming* written in the second century BC. It was intended to be a guide for those buying a farm for the first time rather than a book for experienced farmers, and goes into great detail about how to choose a property and furnish it as well as how to farm it, even to the extent of giving the names of the local towns that were the best suppliers of various items of farm equipment. The advice extends to furniture; when building a farm from scratch, he advised the owner to specify three benches and two seats to be built into the structure, although he does not explain where they should be built, and includes furniture in the extensive lists of equipment required for two 'typical' farms of different sizes. The farms were to be run by managers (who were probably slaves) so while the lists identify the number and types of slaves needed to work the farm, they make no reference to the owner and his family. The inexperienced farmers Cato was writing for would have bought the farm as an investment, not as a way of life and would have visited the farm rather than lived there (*On Farming* 2.1; 142; Dalby 1998, 22). The furniture in the lists is that needed for the everyday use of the farm and does not include anything specifically required by the owner, such as dining-couches.

Furniture for an olive farm of 60 hectares and 13 people (*On Farming*, 10)

1	side-table	*abacum*
2	bronze circular tables	*orbes ahenos*
3	tables	*mensas*
3	large stools/benches	*scamna magna*
1	stool in the bedroom	*scamnum in cubiculo*
3	low stools	*scabilla*
4	seats	*sellas*
2	chairs	*solia*
1	bed in the bedroom	*lectum in cubiculo*
4	beds sprung with leather straps	*lectos loris subtentos*
3	beds	*lectos*
8	mattresses	*culcitos*
8	blankets	*instragula*
16	cushions	*pulvinos*
10	coverlets	*operimenta*
3	towels	*mappas*

The domestic farm equipment included a loom, a pint measure, a bucket for drawing water, a ewer, a small pot, a wash-basin, a tray, a chamber-pot, a watering can with a large spout, a ladle and a candlestick, two iron fire-tongs, an iron fire-shovel and two iron braziers, an iron mortar for pounding wheat, a wooden mortar, a fuller's mortar, two further mortars without specified use, pestles for beans, for wheat, for seeds, and for nuts, a grain measure for a peck and for a half-peck, and a pint measure.

Furniture for a vineyard of 25 hectares and 16 people (*On Farming*, 11)

1	bronze table	
4	beds	
1	stool	
2	tables	
1	side-table	
1	box for clothes	*arcam*
1	storage cupboard	*armarium promptarium*
6	long stools/benches	
1	chair	
4	mattresses	
4	blankets	
6	pillows	
6	coverlets	
3	towels	

In addition, in the press-room there should be a round bronze table, a bench, bedding for two freeborn guards (a third man, a slave, sleeps with 'the press-workers') and a pillow or cushion. Many of the other items of equipment read the same as for the olive farm.

It is difficult to make sense of all of the numbers involved without knowing how many rooms there were in the building and how they were organised, and it is also likely there have been copying mistakes over the years. For example, in the olive farm there are eight beds, eight mattresses, eight blankets, 16 pillows but only ten coverlets: perhaps the 'VI' has been lost from 'XVI' at some stage. In the olive-yard there are eight beds for 13 people, while in the vine-yard apparently four for 16 people, but if some slept on the floor, Cato does not seem to have included the bedding for all of them. In the olive farm the bed and stool or bench for the bedroom presumably belongs to the farm manager and his wife, while the other beds are apparently divided into two qualities, four with leather strapping and three simple beds (perhaps with wooden slats as the mattress support, although with a good mattress the form of support would not be noticed).

Two hundred years later, Columella expanded on Cato's themes and gave his own theories on running a farm. His description of the duties of the manager's wife includes advice on the storage of goods within the farmhouse so that everything was in its correct place and easy to retrieve. As the owners were only expected to be visiting the farm once in a while, most of these items must have been for the use of the slaves running the farm. He says that the most expensive vessels and clothes should be kept in the highest lockable room, and that delicate furniture should be kept in a well-lit room used for those tasks requiring the most light. He suggests separate places for the objects used in religious ceremonies, those items that women required for holidays and those that men required for fighting, the trappings required for ceremonial days and the footwear for both sexes. Military equipment and weapons should be stored elsewhere, as should the equipment required in wool-working. In another place vessels should be kept, divided between those generally used for storing food, those used in bathing, those used for toilette, and those used for everyday meals and those for feasts. Those items used 'on festival days and on the arrival of guests and on certain rare occasions' were to be numbered, handed out, and then counted back in and returned to their correct place. The wife should regularly inspect the furniture and clothing that had been stored away to make sure they had not fallen apart (*On Farming*, 12.3). The store-rooms containing these items must have included shelves, chests and/or cupboards. Separate store-rooms would also be needed for grain, wine, other crops and food preserved in sealed pottery vessels or wooden barrels (*ibid.*, 12.3.2; 12.46-58).

14

Furniture in use: multiple room houses

Literary evidence, scenes in art and some of the houses from settlements round Vesuvius all provide evidence of what furniture was to be found in the different rooms of a house. The evidence is always incomplete, as no Roman author gives a blow-by-blow description of all the furniture present in a certain room, and no artistic representation can show all four walls of a room, but an idea of what items were likely to be used in each room can be built up. For those who could not afford numerous rooms, the available space had to provide multiple uses so that the features of dining-rooms, bedrooms, and studies could be combined into one, in the same way that small modern-built houses often combine kitchen and dining-room, or dining-room and living-room.

Furniture and decoration
It is likely that Roman houses were built with specific uses in mind for most, if not all, of the rooms. A dining-room, for example, had to be planned from the start, to allow enough space to accommodate couches and entertainment space, and in the later period they were even built with curved walls to suit the fashionable semi-circular couches. Bedrooms were often designed with the location of the bed in mind, with an alcove, niche, slightly raised floor or lowered ceiling to indicate their intended position. At other times recesses for beds or dining-couches were cut into the wall at a later date, perhaps when a room changed function (Mols 1999, 125; Allison 2204, fig. 4.2). Wall decoration sometimes also showed a change to fit furniture, although most of the time furniture such as cupboards and beds with boards concealed large areas of painted wall without regard to the design. A bed with boards in the House of Trojan Shrine, Pompeii, is as long as the room is wide, and would have totally hidden the wall-painting on all three sides up to a height of approximately 0.8m (Mols 1999, figs 177-8).

   Mosaics more often show variations in consideration of beds and dining-couches. Dining-rooms often had simple decoration where it would not be seen, and more elaborate mosaics elsewhere, usually orientated so that the best view of them could be had by those dining rather than those entering the room. Despite such evidence of planned room function, the occupants of houses would switch the uses of rooms to suit their own purposes, and were no more bound by the architects' original ideas than occupants of current-day houses are, who use rooms intended as bedrooms or dining-rooms as studies, workrooms, games rooms or similar.

   The houses under consideration are those with enough rooms for there to be specialisation in the rooms, with separate rooms used for dining, cooking, sleeping and so on, unlike the small houses and apartments lower down the social scale. The *atrium* house, although well-known from Pompeii and Herculaneum and often taken as a 'typical' Roman house, was already considered an old-fashioned design by the very early first century AD, and most Roman houses never possessed one (Ellis 2002, 28). The *atrium* is mentioned disproportionately in the following discussion because of the survival of furniture *in situ* in the *atrium* houses of the area round Pompeii. More widespread both in terms of geographic and chronological spread was the peristyle house, where the rooms were set round a peristyle, consisting of an open yard or garden with a colonnade on two or more sides. In cities, particularly in the Mediterranean region, apartments in multi-storeyed buildings were a common form of housing. They ranged from two or three linked rooms to examples with multiple rooms decorated with expensive painted walls and mosaic floors, although on the whole there were less rooms than in the large houses.

   The larger apartments, and the *atrium* and peristyle houses were inward-looking town-houses, while the country villa was designed to be outward-looking to take advantage of the scenic views, but all four types had the same range of room types, and the same furniture requirements. In some cases, the furniture was exactly the same, having been transported between town and country by the owner (Pliny, *Letters*, 3.19.3).

   In the Roman period there was rarely a division between home and work-place and it was perfectly normal for even quite richly appointed houses to have industrial or commercial material within it. Allison's detailed study of 30 *atrium* houses in Pompeii has shown that bulk storage, often in the form of *amphorae*, took place in nine *atria*. Tools such as shovels are found in rooms throughout the houses (Ellis 2002, 107). Colonnades round gardens were also used for storage, and the gardens themselves could contain large produce-bearing trees requiring harvesting rather than ornamental plants (Allison 2004, 69, 90). The House of Polybius, Pompeii, for example, seems to have produced figs, olives, lemons and cherries or pears (Ellis 2002, 163). Pliny saw nothing inappropriate in describing one of the rooms in his luxury Laurentine villa as overlooking 'another well-stocked kitchen garden' (*Letters*, 2.17.15).

Atrium

The *atrium*, in those houses that possessed one, was a hall with a central water-catchment pool (*impluvium*) under an opening in the roof and usually had rooms opening off all four sides. Some scholars believe that the room, as the first that guests reached and therefore part of the 'public' space of the building, would have been furnished to impress, with little clutter in it other than a marble table set up by the *impluvium*, a large strong-box to demonstrate the family wealth and perhaps a shrine to show their piety. It is likely that in reality the room was much more cluttered. It was originally the main working room of the house and continued to be the principal service area used both by the whole household and by visitors. Anyone entering ot leaving the house had to walk through the *atrium*, as did any-one wanting to use the side rooms opening off it, or the rooms at the back of the house. Cupboards and chests containing all sorts of household items (and occasionally strong-boxes) are one of the most common items of furniture found in *atria*, such as the four cupboards found in the House of the Theatrical Pictures (Allison 2004, 69) so members of the household must have frequently been coming in to retrieve items from them throughout the day. In some houses people also worked in the room, the clearest evidence for which are the traces of looms occasionally found set up here. It was a good room for textile-working, as it was provided with good natural light from the opening above the *impluvium* but was relatively sheltered from rain, wind and excessive sun.

Shrines were often built into the structure of the room, with niches or masonry platforms, painted or clad in marble and set with busts and statuettes. Pliny says that cupboards with the wax busts of ancestors were also originally kept in this hall (*Natural Histories*, 35.2.6). Full-size statues seem to be rare, but there was sometimes an elaborate marble table set up to one side of the *impluvium*. This may have originally been a table for holding water pots (below the shallow pool there is usually a deeper cistern, whose mouth was hidden below a cylindrical stone fitting set to one side), but it developed into a display table, often elaborately decorated.

Peristyle

The peristyle could be paved, full of mature, produce-bearing trees or planted with formal gardens and set with fountains. A colonnade, sometimes with a waist-high wall, surrounded the area on two, three or four sides, and there were sometimes open-sided rooms for entertainment opening off the colonnade, taking advantage of the pleasant garden views. In houses with formal gardens, this area was another 'public' part of the house and contained statuary and marble display furniture not intended for use. During good weather, the colonnade was as much living space within the house as more enclosed rooms, shielded from the direct sun if necessary by curtains hung between the columns. In houses based round a peristyle, the colonnade was the major circulation area of the house, with the household members having to use it constantly to move from one room to another as many of the rooms opened directly off it with no other method of access.

In Allison's study, there was evidence for wooden or bronze seats and marble tables in the colonnades round the garden. Like the *atrium*, one of the most common forms of furniture in the colonnades were cupboards and chests, containing a mixture of domestic and utilitarian or industrial material and tools (2003, 88-9). There was also evidence for braziers being used for cooking in the colonnades, either for meals eaten there, in the garden itself, or perhaps in some of the nearby open-fronted rooms used for entertainment.

Dining-room

A dining-room with two or three couches would have been used for all formal evening meals with invited guests, although it is not clear if it would also be used for a family or couple dining alone without guests. The houses of the rich often had more than one dining-room, either for use in different seasons or simply for variety, but certainly as a form of status symbol. Dining-rooms were generally rectangular in shape, although with the rise in popularity of the semi-circular couch, dining-rooms were often built with curved walls to echo the shape of the couch.

The room was always dominated by the dining-couches, which were placed towards the back of the room to leave a large clear space at the front for service and the after-meal entertainment. At Pompeii a typical size for a dining-room is 6 x 4m (Dunbabin 1991, 124), and even in larger rooms set with a row of columns, the space within the columns used for the couches was often not much larger than this, with the extra space apparently used for better access to the couches or for service. The commonality of size is a reflection of the typical nine-place arrangement that does not provide much opportunity for variation in size.

One or more small, portable dining-tables filled the space between the couches. Masonry *triclinia* usually only have one central table for nine diners, but inside more tables could be used: a mosaic from Capua shows at least three tables used with a *triclinium*, and one from Ephesus shows three used with a *stibadium* (Dunbabin 2003, figs 31, 97). The larger scale *triclinia* of the later Roman period, seating about 15 people, would certainly have required more dining-tables.

Elsewhere in the room (it is probable that usually set against a wall), serving-table for drinks (often one-legged), and possibly another for food although perhaps in practise these were often one and the same. There also often have been a side-table used for setting out the items of silver or gold table services not in use.

Marble tables with one leg have been found in association with couches at Herculaneum; as they are not very portable items of furniture they are more likely to have been used as side-tables than dining-tables. Examples were found with beds in the House of the Wooden Partition and in the House with *Cracitum*. In House 11.5 a white marble tabletop supported on a coloured marble support decorated with a Bacchic figure with a garland was found in an upper room with a *biclinium* (Mols 1999, 125, fns 765-6). Another *biclinium* was used in a room with a marble table with a herm on its leg, an upright wooden cupboard and a wall cupboard with bone decoration (*ibid.,* 152).

Another side-table might have been required for a water boiler, an elaborately constructed bronze vessel consisting of a section to hold water and a section to hold charcoal or other fuel within its body (Dunbabin 2003, fig. 98). It was used to produce hot water on tap to be mixed with the wine according to the individual guest's taste. This was a very specific but widespread Roman custom, along with the opposite luxury, the use of snow or very cold water for an extra-cool drink. The vessels could be beautifully made, and were intended for display. They are shown sitting by themselves on a circular three-legged table, a triangular table and an apparent wooden pillar (see *21*, lower; Dunbabin 2003, figs 104, 106, pl. XII).

Depending on the custom of the household, there might also have been high-backed chairs for the women of the family as, traditionally, they were supposed to sit in chairs to eat. 'Women used to dine seated with their reclining men-folk, a custom which made its way from the social gatherings of men to things divine. For at the banquet of Jupiter he himself was invited to dine on a couch, while Juno and Minerva had chairs, a form of austerity which our age is more careful to retain on the Capitol than in its houses, no doubt because it is more important to the commonwealth that discipline be maintained for goddesses than for women' (Valerius Maximus, *Memorable Deeds and Sayings,* 2.12). This fashion certainly spread to the provinces, as can be seen on tombstones from as far apart as France and Palmyra (see *25, 56*; Colledge 1976, pls 98, 100, 102), but was certainly never exclusive.

Some external masonry *triclinia* have built-in benches set at the end of the couches, which might be in imitation of wooden benches in internal dining-rooms. These were probably not a permanent feature of the rooms but brought in as or when necessary. When Terence visited the house of the poet Caecilius to show him his new play, the poet was already dining 'and being meanly dressed, Terence is said to have read the beginning of his play sitting on a bench next to the great man's couch. But after a few lines he was invited to recline at the table' (Suetonius, *On Poets*, 2). In the play *Stichus* by Plautus, when a parasite called Gelasimus, in attempting to get invited to a meal, hears that the host has already filled all nine places, he replies: 'of course I don't expect accommodation on a couch. You know me – I'm a bench man', suggesting extra guests (of low status) could be included in the meal sitting upright (act 3, scene 2, 491). Other hosts sometimes simply squeezed more guests onto the couches, with five per couch seen as a crush (Horace, *Satires* 1.4.86; Cicero, *Against Piso,* 27.67).

Other furniture could be brought in as wanted. Pliny had comfortable chairs brought into the room for a reading after a meal, and a musician has a low rectangular table for her set of musical bowls in an illustration from the *Vienna Genesis* (fig. 20, top). The younger members of the Imperial household who dined with Augustus sat at a separate table, their table and seats presumably being brought in especially for those meals and removed when the room was to be used for more formal dining. Children did not recline to eat. In the Imperial family, Tacitus records that 'it was the regular custom that the children of the Emperors should take their meals in sight of their relatives, seated with other nobles of their age at a more frugal table of their own' (*Annals,* 13.16), while Claudius let children sit on the pillow-rests of the couches 'after the old time custom' (Suetonius, *Claudius,* 32).

It is possible that strong boxes or cupboards with locks were also kept in this room (Ellis 2002, 160).

Lower classes

It was accepted that people of different classes dined in different ways. An inscription from Corfinium records the gift of public feasts and meals by a benefactor, who specified that the town councillors (decurions) should be given 30 *sesterces* while they 'reclined' to eat, the freedman priests of Augustus (*seviri augustales*) 20 *sesterces* while they 'dined' and the plebeians eight *sesterces* while they 'feasted'. Three different verbs were used to describe the process of dining, and although the distinctions cannot be fully understood now, clearly there were accepted differences according to status (Dunbabin 2003, 83). The Armiternium relief shows six men sitting round a small circular dining-table at one such feast (*30*). Columella says that a farm manager (usually a slave) should only recline to eat on holidays, inferring that he must be sitting upright to eat at other times (11.1.19), while in the play *Stichus* slaves refer to having benches and not couches for a feast (Plautus, *Stichus*, act 5, scene 4, 703).

Study, office and library

In *atrium* houses, the room opposite the main entrance between the *atrium* and the peristyle is traditionally identified as the study (*tablinium*), although they are often little more than a wide entrance to the garden with large folding doors to partition them off. Allison's study revealed that these rooms frequently have cupboards and chests in them containing utilitarian items for food preparation and needlework, or items for serving food and drink. Some also had evidence of bedding, but none in her sample had archival material (2003, 80-2; 168).

Whilst this type of room may not have been used as the office, somewhere in all types of *atrium* and peristyle houses there must have been a room for the house archives (in poorer quarters this was probably housed in chests stored in a bedroom). These would include numerous legal documents, correspondence, accounts and family records, including, according to Pliny 'the books of records and written memorials of official careers' (*Natural Histories*, 35.2.7). Fiction and non-fiction books, either in the form of scrolls or codices, might have been kept with the other paperwork although those rich or literate enough to possess large numbers could keep them in separate rooms used as libraries. The library was sometimes used as the place to gather before a meal, to play board games, read or debate (Rossiter 1991, 200-1). Both chests and cupboards could be used to hold paperwork. The room might also hold a desk and straight-backed chair, particularly useful when dealing with large quantities of money (see *37*).

Bedroom

The bedroom, perhaps better described as a 'retiring room' (Ellis 2002, 156) was not seen solely as a place for sleeping, and was often also used as a study and a meeting place for private conversations, similar in a way to a teenager's bedroom today. The major piece of furniture would of course be the bed, usually with a foot-stool. There would also be a seat of some type, either a simple stool, or a high-backed chair for a woman to use while having her hair done or her make-up applied. In the novel *Golden Ass,* Lucius had a small table set with food near his bed (2.16), and while this may have been brought in for the occasion, a table of some type must have been needed in the bedroom for holding the items necessary for a woman's toilette. These would have included perfumes, hair pins, jewellery-boxes, mirrors and the 'boxes and the thousand colours' of cosmetics (Ovid, *Art of Love* 209-10; *Remedies of Love*, 351-4). It is unlikely the woman sat in front of the table as with a modern dressing-table (as for a start, mirrors were hand-held), and it was probably just a low table used to hold the items not currently being used by the slaves as they attended their mistress sitting in her wicker chair elsewhere in the room.

Vessels such as a jug and bowl for washing were often kept on the floor. A first-century bronze mirror shows a bedroom scene with a bed, in front of which and/or under it are a folding stool, a foot-stool with the slippers resting on top, and a basin and jug. Hanging on the wall is a triptych painting, and there is a hanging bowl suspended from the ceiling. A scene from a brothel also shows the jug and basin on the floor near the bed (see *12*), the combination of vessels suggesting a use for washing. Missing is the chamber-pot, which would have been a common feature in most if not all bedrooms.

The use of the bedroom for meetings meant that chairs for guests were often included. Pliny describes a bedroom in one of his country villas as having 'folding doors opening onto the arcade and a window looking out on to the sea. Opposite the dividing wall was an extremely elegant section which can become part of the room one moment by drawing back the glass doors and curtains, and at the next divided from it by closing them. It holds a couch and two high-backed chairs (*cathedras*)' (*Letters*, 2.17.21).

Chests for storing clothes may have been included in the bed-room, although it is possible in larger houses clothes could have been stored elsewhere and brought in as required. Examples from Herculaneum show that the chests could also be used for more general storage. One found in a room with a bed in the House of the Two *Atria* contained correspondence and food (Mols 1999, 125, fn. 766). A first-floor room, towards the rear of the House of the Wooden Shrine, contained a bed, a wooden bench and three chests, one of which contained wax tablets and one pottery and bronze vessels (*ibid.,* 183). Cupboards are sometimes found in bedrooms, as are shrines, both wall-mounted or combined with another item of furniture (*ibid.*, 125, fn 766). A shrine/cupboard found in a room with a bed and a wooden table contained a bronze statuette of Hercules and a marble statuette of a goddess, possibly Venus (*ibid.*, 193).

Living-room

This is more a concept than a recognisable room in a house-plan as it is in modern times. It may not be just a single room, but a selection of different rooms chosen according to the season, weather or whim of the house-owners. The term is taken to describe the space used by the family when they were on their own, without guests to impress, perhaps dining alone, or sitting together during the evening. A tomb wall-painting from the Necropolis of the Via Laurentina, Ostia, shows one possible scene (*colour plate 16*). The deceased is shown reclining on a wide bed with boards, with a footstool beneath it. Placed centrally in front of the bed is a wicker chair with its own foot-stool, and towards the head of the bed is a three-legged dining table. Just beyond this end of the couch is an ornate metal candelabra, while at the other end stands a tall decorated cupboard.

73 Kitchen fittings. Mosaic, Marbella, Spain

Kitchen

Kitchens often had built-in masonry benches for charcoal fires or enclosed ovens. In Allison's study of *atria* houses the raised benches were 0.6–1m high, 0.5–1.35m wide and 0.75–3.25m long (2003, 99). Some kitchens had permanent tanks for water storage (Stefani 2005, 153), sometimes with built-in drains. Another very common fixed feature was a toilet, probably also used to dispose of the waste water produced in a kitchen (Allison 2003, 99). When not in the kitchen itself, toilets were often in rooms close by, or fitted into the space under staircases, and were little more than a wooden seat set over a cess pit or a drain. Some kitchens had a niche in the wall, some of which may have been used for storage and others as shrines; other rooms just had shrines (*lararia*) painted onto a wall. Their presence in the kitchen is probably related to their connection with the household hearth.

A villa in Marbella, Spain, has an unusual border to the black and white geometric mosaic in the colonnade round a courtyard that shows a selection of kitchen implements (*73*; the rows are divisions in the illustration only and appear in the mosaic as one continuous band). On the short end of the colonnade are implements connected with bathing; either each side of the mosaic had items belonging to different themes (the whole border no longer survives), or else bathing equipment was also stored in the kitchen. The bathing equipment (*73*, top row) consists of slippers, a rack with a hanging dish and implements, three strigils, two water dishes, a small cupboard possibly for oils, and a large open bowl with its ladle. The kitchen items start with a trestle table holding a rack of ribs, a rabbit, a trussed chicken, a fish, snails, eggs and a large meat cleaver. This is followed by objects identified as two mixing bowls with their pestles, a ladle, and a poker for the fire (second row), a tripod, a brush, another poker, a grid-iron and a baker's peel or shovel for the ashes. Next, set side-wards because of the lack of depth to the narrow border, there is a conical sieve hanging from a framework above a bowl (third row).

Next is an *amphora* (of a type usually used for transporting fish sauce), another vessel possibly representing the type of *amphora* used to transport olive oil, and a jug. Hanging from some pegs on a board fixed to the wall are a bird, another joint of ribs and a bundle of herbs or vegetables (fourth row). Next is another large bowl with a ladle, and then a table holding a flagon and cups. There is then an openwork rack, either for suspending from the ceiling or for attachment to a wall, holding three song birds threaded onto a loop and two fish (fifth row). The next image is probably a basket containing vegetables such as leeks, and then a hot water heater, with fuel beside it. After a gap in the mosaic (large enough to contain two or three other items) there is a large openwork container, possibly used to hold birds, and a large basin (sixth row). The end of the border is also missing.

This mosaic shows one table for holding containers for liquids (necessary for having water handy when there was no running water in the room), and a work-table for dealing with food. Meat is shown hanging up in the open and not in a meat safe, although this may be the result of suspended food being more artistic than a featureless cupboard (see also *colour plate. 17*).

Many of the items must have been stored on shelves or in cupboards, both built-in and freestanding (*60*, middle, from kitchen; Allison 2003, 100).

Bath-suites

Bath-suites connected to private houses were rarely such grand affairs as the public bath-houses, consisting usually of a few, small interconnecting rooms. A room containing a plunge-bath built against one wall with connecting doors in two different walls leading to other rooms did not leave much space for any furniture. Sidonius, describing his house in a letter to a friend, touches on this problem, recording that 'the bath-chamber itself has its area perfectly adjusted by the nicest measurements so as to find room for as many chairs as the semi-circular bath usually admits bathers, without causing the slaves to get in one another's way' (*Letters*, 2.2).

Images of families on the way to the baths show slaves carrying clothes, boxes, containers and candlesticks, so little seems to have been stored in the suite itself. Portable seats, such as the iron folding stool shown in the bath-house mosaic at Piazza Armerina (see *50*), and possibly also the folding chair (see *59*) were probably used to get round the problem of space, being brought out only when needed. Tables for food or board games were presumably also brought in as and when necessary. Despite the presence of water and drains, latrines are rarely found in bath-suites (Allison 2004, 137).

Slave-quarters

The way that a rich Roman house was run probably has no close parallels in the western world. The evidence suggests that there was not one entrance for the family and one for the slaves as with the tradesmen entrances of the Victorian upper-class house, and door porters in Roman houses were needed as much to keep an eye on who was leaving the house as who was entering it; the slaves of the fictional Trimalchio clearly left by the front door as there was a sign beside it reading 'no slave to go out of doors except by the master's orders. Penalty: one hundred stripes'. (Petronius, *Satyricon*, 28).

Extremely rich Romans could have a huge number of slaves in their house that needed to be accommodated. When the city prefect Pedanius Secundus was murdered by one of his own slaves, a law that decreed the whole slave household living under the same roof should be punished meant that 400 slaves were executed (Tacitus, *Annals*, 42-5). In such large households, there may have been specially built quarters for the slaves, and some buildings with multiple small rooms have been identified as slave accommodation, although they can also be interpreted as brothels or inns (George 1997, 17, figs 1-2).

In more modest establishments, there is little evidence that rooms used by slaves were kept separate from the rest of the house in the nineteenth-century way of locating those rooms most used by servants on entirely separate floors to those rooms used by the family, so that kitchens were in the basement ('below stairs') and their bedrooms were in the attics. While there were some parts of the house that must have been used primarily by slaves, such as the kitchens, there are rarely clearly defined 'service' areas within the house, and in some houses even the kitchen opened off the *atrium* (Allison 2003, 136). Slaves would have been visible working in the public areas of the house, as any looms set up in the *atrium* would usually have been worked by slaves. Everyday domestic items used by slaves were stored in cupboards and chests in public areas, and any commercial activities carried out in the houses would have involved the presence of slaves.

In the nineteenth century, female servants stayed for only approximately three years before moving on (either in search of a better situation, or retiring to get married), producing a constantly changing, transient household (Flanders 2003, 96). In a Roman household, although slaves could be bought and sold at whim, the best slaves were considered to be those who had been born and brought up in the house, and were therefore a long-term part of the household. Even when freed, ex-slaves could also continue to live in or use the house. The quality of the space given to slaves would depend on the type of slave, with educated slaves or those who helped to run large households being given better quarters than lowly kitchen slaves, water-carriers or hypocaust-stokers. Some of Pliny's slaves had rooms equal to those allocated to freedmen, and of a quality suitable to be offered to guests as the need arose, and were apparently not so far away from the room he used as his personal library (*Letters*, 2.17.9). When Nero was trying to escape at the end of his reign, his party crawled on all fours through a tunnel dug through a wall to get into a villa unseen, ending up resting in the first small room they came to, which belonged to a slave. While the bed with just 'a common mattress' and a mantle for a blanket may not have been suitable for an Emperor, it reveals that at least some slaves slept on a proper bed, and not on a masonry base or on the floor (Suetonius, *Nero,* 48.4). The doorkeeper of the imperial house at Rome also had a bed to go with his mattress, as another fleeing Emperor, Vitellius, found when he took refuge in his room and used it as a barrier against the door (Suetonius, *Vitellius,* 16).

Other slaves seem to have slept on mattresses or mats on the floor that could be cleared away during the day. Ovid, when listing ways of gaining the favour of a woman in his book *The Art of Love*, includes winning over 'him who lies before the door to her inner chamber' (2.260), and when the slave Fotis visits Lucius in his guest bedroom in the novel *The Golden Ass*, Lucius records that bedding for his slaves had been made up 'on the ground some distance from the threshold, to keep them from overhearing the sounds of our love-making' (2.16). It is likely slaves also slept on temporary bedding in other rooms, such as the kitchen (certainly a common location for servants in later centuries), although there must have been somewhere for those without fixed bedrooms to store their personal belongings, including, at the very least, outdoor cloaks or other clothes not currently being worn.

The worst slave accommodation would have been that provided by the chained slaves used on some farms in the early Roman period. Columella describes a villa with winter and summer apartments for the owners, and discusses the direction that rooms such as the bedrooms and dining-rooms should face in order to benefit from the sun or shade, before continuing to the rooms used by slaves: 'it will be best for that the rooms for unfettered slaves be built to admit the midday sun at the equinox; for those who are in chains there should be an underground chamber, as wholesome as possible, receiving light through a number of narrow windows built so high from the ground that they cannot be reached with the hand', where presumably large numbers of slaves slept together with minimum furnishings or possessions. Columella also suggests that the farmhouse should have 'a spacious and high kitchen, that the rafters may be free from the dangers of fire, and that it may offer a convenient stopping place for the slave household at every season of the year', suggesting this room was the natural gathering place for the slaves (*On Farming*, 1.6.3).

15

Furniture in use: the rich

Descriptions of the houses of the rich tend to concentrate on the number of rooms and their uses rather than the furniture within them. It was common for rich people to have duplicate rooms, such as multiple dining-rooms and bedrooms that they could use as the fancy took them. Suetonius thought it noteworthy enough to remark that Augustus 'used the same bedroom in winter and summer for more than forty years' (*Augustus*, 72.1). Another Roman who was not impressed by the habit of changing bedrooms, was Seneca, who asked: 'What's the good of multiple bedrooms? You lie in one' (*Letters*, To Lucilius, 89).

Pliny the Younger provides room by room descriptions of two of his villas, but mentions only a few items of furniture in passing. His description of his Tuscan villa (*Letters*, 5.6) mentions four dining-rooms (one of which is a garden *stibadium*), 13 bedrooms, a bath-suite and four further 'suites' of rooms not identified in any greater detail. The house includes 'an informal dining-room where I entertain personal friends' and a bedroom where 'no daylight, voice, nor sound can penetrate'. His Laurentine villa (*Letters*, 2.17) had at least 27 rooms, consisting of three dining-rooms, six bedrooms, a room that could be used either as a moderately-sized dining-room or a large bedroom, a bath-suite and at least 17 other rooms, including an *atrium*, courtyard and inner hall, a library, a sun-room, and rooms kept for the use of his slaves and freedmen.

He also had a suite of rooms that included three bedrooms built at the end of a long arcade with windows that led away from the main house towards the sea. One of these was for use at night 'where I cannot hear the young slaves, the sea or storms'. He retired to this suite 'especially during the Saturnalia when the rest of the roof resounds with festive cries in the holiday freedom, for I am not disturbing my household's merry-making, nor they my studies'. The decoration, presence of folding doors and large windows, and rooms which were sheltered or quiet or which received the sun were of more importance to Pliny than the quality of the furniture within them.

In the *Satyricon*, Petronius' description of a dinner party held by the rich freedman Trimalchio mentions a few items of furniture, although since he is making fun of a man with more money than taste, it is a pity that he did not describe the dining-room furniture in as much detail as he mentions the elaborate food. In the *atrium* there was a shrine, and possibly also the strong box mentioned during the meal, which was large enough to hold the 10 million *sesterces* returned when it could not be invested. In one of the dining-rooms (the house had four on the ground floor, and another on an upper floor), Petronius mentions a water-clock and a side-table holding dishes of food. The dining-tables removed between two courses were replaced by another set rather be cleaned. For another course, cloths covered with images of the tools of the hunt were draped over the couches, and one of the guests jokes that Trimalchio was so rich even the stuffing in the mattresses was dyed purple and red. After a break for a session in the bath-suite, the guests were taken to a different dining-room, where Trimalchio's wife Fortunata had laid out her treasures, including tables of solid silver.

Clement of Alexandria's list of some of the luxuries that should be given up by Christians included 'vessels of silver and gold, some for serving food and others for uses which I am ashamed to name, made of pieces of cedar, citrus and ebony, and tripods of ivory, and couches made up of ivory pieces with feet of silver, and bed-boards decorated with gold and tortoiseshell, and bed-clothes of purple and other colours difficult to produce' (*The Instructor,* 2.3). He tells his readers to 'have the strength to banish magnificent bedding, gold-woven pillows, bed-clothes of an alternating smooth and gold design, of shell-fish purple, of athlete's wraps, and the most expensive Eastern furs, and poet's mantles of purple, and soft and luxurious clothes, and beds softer than sleep' (*ibid.*, 2.9).

When the furniture of rich people *is* mentioned, it is most frequently couches and dining-tables, so it is clear that the quality of the furniture that would be seen by guests was of the utmost importance. According to Plutarch, 'when the rich man dines alone with his wife or intimates he lets his tables of citrus-wood and golden cups rest in peace and he uses common furnishings, and his wife attends without her gold and purple, dressed in plain attire' (*Moralia, On the Love of Wealth*, 528). Juvenal remarked that the rich 'get no pleasure from eating … unless the enormous round table top rests on a massive piece of ivory, a rampart snarling leopard …. To these people a table leg made of silver is the equivalent of an iron ring [of the type worn by plebeians] on their finger' (*Satires*, 11.120-9). In literature, the same elements come up again and again; ivory couches, citrus-wood tables, purple covers, and extensive silver services.

Imperial furniture

The degree of pomp used in the Imperial household changed from Emperor to Emperor. The Emperors were 'classified with either the good or the bad emperors' in the series of biographies collected together as the *Scriptores Historiae Augustae* (*Verus,* 1.2). Good emperors were usually seen as being modest and frugal while bad emperors were extravagant and luxurious. Any description of their household furniture or furnishings often depends on this simplistic classification, and so is therefore biased towards the two extremes. In most cases the furniture in the Imperial houses would be no different in quality or design to that owned by other very rich men.

In the court of Severus Alexander, according to a biographer who approved of him, he was not to be called 'lord' (*dominus*), but simply to be greeted by name ('*ave, Alexander*'), while any-one who bowed his head or said anything flattering was ejected (*SHA,* 18.1). Gallienus, on the other hand, gave those who kissed his hand four gold coins (*SHA The Two Gallieni* 17.6). To show respect 'good' emperors stood up to greet consuls or members of the Senate while 'bad' ones remained seated (*ibid.; Hadrian,* 8.11, 21.4; *Carus, Carinus and Numerian* 17.2), and although the staff of Severus Alexander had to stand while he was at work signing letters, he did allow those in bad health to sit (*SHA,* 4.1-3).

The seat of the Emperor (not called a throne, as this was an attribute of kings), while not supposed to be used by any-one else, was obviously not very distinctive in appearance. When Septimius Severus came to Rome for the first time as a young man, he not only came to an Imperial banquet wearing normal dining-clothes when he should have worn a toga and so had to borrow one from the Emperor, he also 'sat down in the Imperial chair which an attendant had carelessly left accessible, being quite unaware that this was not allowed' (*SHA Septimius Severus,* 1.7-9). With the benefit of hindsight these were seen as omens of his future position as Emperor, rather than embarrassing mistakes by a young man.

Hadrian or Elagabalus had introduced table-cloths decorated with gold or made from cloth of gold, while Gallienus always used table-cloths of gold (*mantelibus: SHA Severus Alexander* 37.2; *SHA The Two Gallieni,* 16.3). The Imperial furnishings auctioned off by Marcus Aurelius included couch-covers of gold-woven cloth, some of which were bought by Elagabalus before he became emperor. He became the first commoner to use such covers, but the fact that the Emperor himself sold them shows that there was nothing to stop people outside the Imperial family using such extravagant furnishings if they had the money to pay for them (*SHA Elagabalus,* 19.1).

The Emperors kept a shrine either in their bedroom or had a separate room nearby which acted as a shrine. There was a golden 'royal' statue of Fortuna 'which was customarily carried about with the Emperors and placed in their bedroom' (*SHA Antonius Pius*, 12.5; *Severus*, 23.5), but they also selected their own statuettes. First thing in the morning, Severus Alexander 'if it were permissible, that is to say, if he had not lain with his wife ... would worship in the *lararium*, in which he kept statues of the deified Emperors ... and also of certain holy souls, among them Apollonius and, according to a contemporary writer, Christ, Abraham, Orpheus and others of the same character, besides the portraits of his ancestors' (*SHA Severus Alexander*, 29.2). Hadrian had a statuette of Augustus as a child, while Marcus Aurelius had gold statues of his teachers (*SHA Deified Augustus*, 7.1; *Marcus Aurelius*, 3.5).

16

Furniture in use: non-domestic furniture

Bath-houses and bath-suites

Public bath-houses could be massive buildings. Two of the largest examples in Rome were the Baths of Caracalla at 27 acres and the Baths of Diocletian at 32 acres. Each was capable of holding huge numbers of people. They were places of entertainment where getting clean was almost secondary to spending sociable hours with friends. There were built-in hot and cold plunge-baths and swimming pools, and sometimes wooden tubs suitable for use by a single person. Celsus recommends patients recovering from some operations to relax in such a tub 'leaning back in the hot water so that the water covers him from his knees to his navel' (*On Medicine*, 7.26.5). Contemporary descriptions of other bath-house activities include massages, hair-removal, board-games, gossiping and snacking, implying the need for stools, tables and some form of massage-table available for the use of the patrons.

Stone benches set against the walls were common in changing-rooms, and free-standing benches in the heated rooms. Nigidius Vaccula donated a brazier and benches to the Forum Baths in Pompeii, and an inscription from Italy records a woman called Alfia Quarta who had built a bath-house for women at her own expense who also equipping it with a bronze *labrum* (hot water basin), brazier and seats (*CIL* IX, no. 3677). Vitruvius recommended benches set in apses round the exercise yard 'where the philosophers, rhetoricians and others who delight in study, may sit and dispute' (*On Architecture*, 5.11.2). Larger bath-houses in urban centres could have libraries and rooms for lectures, poetry and music, which would also have been furnished with benches, and Martial refers to a cook-shop with 'seats' set up within a bath-house (*Epigrams*, 5.70.3).

Mosaics show low rectangular tables used to hold bathing equipment and athlete's prizes (see *40*), and sets of shelves or cupboards may have been required for equipment owned by the establishment. Patrons could also bring not only their own bathing equipment, but their own furniture, which was a practise deplored by the early church father Clement of Alexandria: 'High-backed chairs decorated with gold and silver, and innumerable vessels of gold and silver, some for drinking, some for eating and others for bathing are carried round with [the women]. There are also charcoal grid-irons, for they have arrived at such a pitch of self-indulgence that they eat and drink while bathing. And articles of silver with which they make a show, they ostentatiously set out in the baths, and thus display their wealth out of excessive pride …. proving at least that they themselves cannot meet and sweat without a multitude of vessels, although poor women who have no display equally enjoy their baths' (*The Instructor*, 3.5).

Bars and inns

Bars, for serving hot food and drinks, often had an outer room open to the street with a straight, an L- or a U-shaped masonry bar. Examples at Pompeii frequently have stepped masonry shelves built into the short end of the bar connecting to the wall, while at Ostia the shelves were often a separate structure built behind and parallel to the bar. A relief from Ostia shows these shelves being used to store cups (*74*). The third-century Inn of Alexander Helix at Ostia had a large room with at least two entrances to the streets and a central water-tank that may have been a fountain. About a quarter of the room was taken up by a bar projecting into the room that had a hearth and a set of three shelves behind it. The masonry fittings were all covered with marble veneer, and there were figured black and white mosaics on the floor. A door led through to a smaller inner room which may have been set up with seats and tables for those who wanted to eat. This inner room is a common feature of inns, although the size of some of the rooms would have made them cramped and easily crowded.

Scenes of tavern life painted on the walls of the bars give an idea of how the bars were used. A set of paintings from tavern VI, 14, 36 at Pompeii include images of men sitting on stools being served with drinks by a woman and two men playing a board game. The captions record accusations of cheating, and the landlord telling them to take the resulting fight outside (Ward-Perkin and Claridge 1976, cat. 227). Other paintings from a tavern on the Road of Mercury shows a group of four people gathered round a three-legged dining-table (*colour plates 17-8*). They are all sitting upright, as befits their social standing, and although they are shown drinking, one scene shows an overhead rack hung with food suggesting that food was also available.

More formal dining could also be had at inns. The Inn of Sittius at Pompeii had a sign advertising a dining-room with three couches (Jashemski 1979, 172), while others had garden *triclinia* (*ibid.*, fig. 250, 261). A building on the outskirts of Pompeii

74 Tavern scene with counter and rectangular table. Stone relief, Ostia

had a series of five masonry *triclinia* set in private rooms overlooking the peristyle and enclosed by wooden lattices, presumably for private parties (*ibid.*, fig. 266).

Shops

Shops were generally small, single rooms, often with a wooden shutter for the street wall so that it could be opened up fully to make maximum use of the available space and to attract buyers (Ellis 2002, 78, fig. 14, pl. 7). There were tables (both wooden and stone) or built-in masonry counters where the goods could be displayed (*75*) or a desk for examining goods, which could also be used for counting money and doing the accounts (see *37*, lower). Other goods, such as meat or cloth-products, were hung from hooks on the wall or beams suspended from the ceiling, or else stacked on shelves. Small sets of shelves could sit on the table or counter, or be hung on the wall, while tall sets stood on the floor against the wall. Martial refers to scrolls kept in pigeonholes in a book shop (with advertisements covering its doorposts; *Epigrams*, 1.117) while a friend of Sidonius had so many books he said it was like looking at the shelves of a professional scholar or the tall cupboards of a book-seller (*Letters*, 2.9). Benches or settles were supplied for the use of the more honoured customers. A wall painting from Pompeii showing a felt-maker's shop depicts a tall wooden table covered with a table-cloth laid with objects on display set in front of a second table or counter, which has a small set of wooden shelves at one end of it. The shop-keeper stands behind this second table and a patron sits on a settle to one side (*75*).

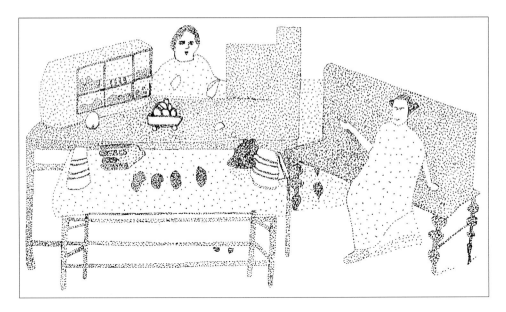

75 Felt-maker's shop. Wall painting, Pompeii

Martial describes a rich man visiting a luxury furniture workshop, which apparently had space enough for displaying a number of large items of furniture: 'he stripped the coverings from round table tops and called for the oiled ivory [legs] exhibited aloft [to be brought down]; and after measuring a tortoiseshell couch for six diners four times, lamented that it was not large enough for his citrus wood table' (*Epigrams*, 9.59.7-10). Workshops for manufactured goods were usually part of the same building as the shop selling the finished articles, as were the living quarters for the family.

Law courts

Law courts were impermanent establishments, set up as necessary in the town *forum* or basilica, or even lecture-halls and record-offices (Tacitus, *Dialogues on Oratory*, 39 1) They were often noisy and theatrical places. Four courts were held at the same time in the Basilica Iulia in Rome, so the speeches of a loud-voiced advocate or the cheers and clapping of the audience (paid or otherwise) in one court could be heard in the others (Quintilian, *The Education of an Orator, 12.5*). Quintilian also lists a number of ways of 'moving the court to tears', including having the accused dressed in mourning, bringing in their aged parents or young children, making good use of the evidence such as blood-stained swords and bone taken from wounds, showing paintings of the crime, and getting the accused to throw himself at the feet of the judges and clasp their knees in supplication (*ibid.*, 6.30-5). Benches were used for the two opposing parties, their lawyers and the witnesses, forming a rough circle in front of the judges who used benches or chairs of state, while the audience, free to come and go at will, stood further back (Suetonius, *Augustus* 56.3; Cicero, *For Milo* 1.1). Nero laid down a law that people should pay 'a fixed and reasonable fee for the services of their advocates but nothing at all for the benches, which were to be furnished free of charge by the public treasury' (Suetonius, *Nero*, 17). The word 'bench' (*subsellium*) could be used in the abstract as short-hand for the judiciary as a whole, as it is today.

The curia

When the Senate met in their hall (the *curia*) in the Forum at Rome, the consuls sat on their *sellae curulis* on a raised tribune at one end, while the senators sat on benches set on three steps on either side of the room (Cicero, *Philippics,* 5; Suetonius, *Claudius,* 23; *SHA Elagabalus*, 4.2; *Caracalla*, 2.11). When Tiberius's son died, 'the consuls were seated on the ordinary benches as a sign of mourning; he reminded them of their dignity and their place' and they returned to their *sellae curulis*.

Theatre, amphitheatre and circus

Benches were used where a large number of people needed to be seated. In theatres and similar venues, wooden benches (or individual seats for the rich) were used, although a reference to poor people using cushions stuffed with reed suggests some people sat on the stone steps (Martial, *Epigrams,* 14.160). During Nero's reign, people in a theatre used the broken benches as weapons when fighting broke out (Suetonius, *Nero*, 26). The Small Theatre at Pompeii has stone steps 0.7m wide for most of the auditorium, while the steps reserved for the important people (divided from the rest by a low wall) were 0.8m wide. As most seats had a front-to-back depth in the region of 0.4m, this allowed space for the feet on the same step. Ovid even mentions the use of a foot-stool, when he explains how to pick up women in the Circus: 'Sit next to your lady, none will prevent you; sit side by side as close as you can: and it is good that the rows compel closeness, like it or not .... Look round to see that whoever is sitting behind you is not pressing his knees against her tender back. Frivolous minds are won by trifles; many have found useful the deft arranging of a cushion, or to set a foot-stool beneath a dainty foot' (*Art of Love,* 1.135-62).

Temple and church

In the early Roman period larger temples sometimes held a special cushioned couch or seat (*pulvinar*) for the use of the deities set before their altar or statue (the term was later also used of seats of honour for humans, such as the Emperor's seat at the amphitheatre). In the Republican religious ceremony called the *lectisternum* images of the gods were reclined on the couches and food set before them. Temples were probably otherwise reasonably empty of furniture, although small iron candlesticks that appear to be connected with temple sites in Britain must have had tables or shelves to sit on. Offerings were also presumably sometimes set on tables rather than just left on the floor.

In churches, the clergy sat on benches, while a bishop sat on a high-backed seat adopted from the wicker chair (Augustine, *Letters*, 33(ep.126); 47 (ep.209)). A sixth-century ivory example originally given to the archbishop Maximianus has been reconstructed from scattered fragments and is now in Ravenna. It originally had 27 carved panels with detailed images of saints, scenes in the life of Jesus and of Joseph set between strips of richly inhabited scrolls (Bustacchini undated, 80, fig. 1). The altar at one end of the church took the form of a rectangular serving-table.

MILITARY FURNITURE

The upper ranks of the military would have had living quarters equivalent in style and furnishing to those available to civilians of the same status. As a result, houses based on Mediterranean-style town-houses were built in forts throughout the Empire. There was very little difference between these and their civilian counterparts. When stationed in forts, the rank-and-file lived eight infantrymen to a two-room apartment or three cavalrymen to one room, and had a more specialised way of living.

First-century writers tended to imply that the army was conservative. Pliny records that 'people in old times had bedding of straw, in the same way as in camp now' (*Natural Histories*, 8.73.193), and eating was by portion rather than the sophistication of formal dining where the guests could choose both what dishes they tried and how much they ate. Plutarch recorded that in an after-dinner discussion of set portions compared to meals where guests could decide what to eat, the general consensus of opinion was that portions were seen as 'unsociable and vulgar'. 'Even now at sacrifices and public banquets, because of the simplicity and frugality of the fare, each guest is still served his equal portion of the meal'. The conclusion to the discussion was that: 'those portion-banquets of Homer we must not introduce here from the military messes of the camps' (*Moralia, Table-talk 2*, question 10). This method of eating is also suggested in Varro's explanation of the origins of the word for 'table' (*mensa*): 'The eating-table they used to call a *cilliba*. It was square, as even now it is in military camps; the name *cilliba* came from *cibus* (food) [in fact it came from the Greek for 'three-legged table']. Afterwards it was made round, and a possible reason for it being called *mensa* is because it was called *medius* (middle) by us and 'middle' by the Greeks, unless it is because most of the food placed on it was *mensa* (measured out)' (*On the Latin Language*, 5.118). The rectangular table was used most by people sitting up to dine, in particular in taverns and at public banquets where set meals were more likely to be consumed.

There were not separate mess halls in Roman camps as the cooking was not done in bulk. Each group of eight soldiers who shared quarters (consisting of two rooms called a *contubernium*) did their own cooking and eating in their living quarters. Officers, whose status gave them more living space, were more likely to dine reclining. The Commanding Officer in charge of a military unit was generally a member of the minor aristocracy so the size and design of the house would have reflected his status, and would have included a large *triclinium* for formal dining with guests (see *17*). This was often the largest reception room in the house, although some houses were also provided with both summer and winter dining-rooms.

Rank-and-file soldiers may have slept on mattresses on the floor which could be cleared away during the day to provide more space, or else they may have shared beds, although it can be difficult to fit enough beds into the available floor space. There is no evidence they slept in bunk-beds, which solve the space problem but which are a relatively modern invention adapted from sleeping-quarters in ships and railway carriages.

The social status of soldiers suggests they used benches and stools for their seating. The Emperor is usually shown sitting on a folding stool when with the army, and it is likely he is using a type of seat frequently used by soldiers (Wanscher 1980, 155, 157). One of the iron double-folding stools from Hungary was found in a soldier's grave (see *48*), and bronze fittings probably from a folding stool have been found at the forts of both Newstead and Corbridge (Allason-Jones and Bishop 1988, fig. 95).

The number of box fittings (including locks) found on military sites suggests boxes and chests were used for storing personal items. A hoard of military equipment found at Corbridge Roman fort had been buried in a chest 0.9m x 0.6m x 0.4m made of alder-wood. It had iron hinges, lock-plate and right-angled strips at the corners fastened with copper-alloy studs. The whole chest had an outer leather covering (*ibid.*, 95-6; cover). Looked at purely from a space point of view, the smaller boxes are more likely to have been used by soldiers and large chests by officers, or for holding unit-wide possessions such as tools or paperwork.

FUNERARY USE OF FURNITURE

The funeral

For the majority of people, death would take place in their own bed, in their own home. Sarcophagi, for example, depict the dead lying on beds with boards with footstools below (sometimes complete with slippers) and a large basin nearby, probably used for washing (Huskinson 1996, pl.3). These scenes are usually depicting the *conclamatio*, when family and friends gathered round and called out the dead person's name to make sure they were indeed dead and to lament their passing. The family are shown sitting on stools or wicker chairs beside the bed, while other mourners, shown with loose hair and raising their hands in grief, stand.

After the *conclamatio*, the body was then washed, anointed with perfumed oils, dressed, and laid out in state until the funeral could be arranged (Toynbee 1971, 44). For those lower down the social scale, the body must have been laid out on the bed they used in life, but richer people probably used a funerary bed (*lectis funebris*), which was either an existing piece of furniture of suitable quality or a specially made bed that could be burnt with the corpse. When Agrippina was killed on the orders of her son, the Emperor Nero, she was buried in haste so those responsible had to make do with what was available: 'she was cremated the same night [as her murder], on a dining-couch, and with the humblest rites' (Tacitus, *Annals,* 14.9). A relief on the Tomb of the Haterii, Rome, shows a woman lying in state on a bed with boards. Two thick mattresses with striped covers mean that the body is almost level with the top of the boards, while her wreathed head rests on a large pillow with a narrow, fringed cloth draped across it. Mourners stand round the bed, and a man holds out another flower garland to the corpse (Kleiner 1992, 166).

When the funeral details had been arranged, the corpse was carried in a procession from its home to the cemetery, which would have been situated on or near roads leading out of cities and settlements, since burial inside was forbidden by law. The body was transported on a bier, which at its simplest was just a board with four carrying poles, although some were made more elaborate by having a decorative canopy overhead. The bodies of paupers were sometimes put on the bier naked as clothes were expensive and could be re-sold (Martial, *Epigrams* 9.2.12;), while others were wrapped in a linen cloth as a shroud (as shown in images of the raising of Lazarus: Weitzmann 1977, pl. 29), or in re-used cloth such as the brightly striped blanket or curtain used on a corpse at Dura-Europos, Syria (Pfister and Bellinger 1945, cat. 116, pl. XVI). Others were put in a coffin for burial, which was probably also carried to the cemetery on a bier. In the early Roman period, when cremation was the main burial rite, the rich were laid out on a couch that was then carried on the bier. The couch and body were taken off the bier, placed on the pyre and burnt.

A first-century relief from Amiternum, Italy shows a funerary procession in progress, with grieving family, musicians, funeral organiser, and mourners (some of whom may have been professional; Kleiner 1992, fig. 88). Eight men carry the bier, which appears to have a canopy decorated with stars and the moon, although in the relief it appears more as a vertical hanging behind the couch. Eight men were needed for the bier because of the extra weight of the couch; a pauper's body was carried on a bier by four slaves (Martial, *Epigrams* 8.75). On the bier is a bed with *fulcra,* one at each end, with a long, low foot-stool underneath as if it were a bedroom couch. This couch also has two mattresses, with two thin pillows, and the dead man is arranged propped up on one elbow.

At the top of the social scale, Emperors had very elaborate funerals. Julius Caesar, as Dictator, was cremated on an ivory couch spread with purple and gold cloth, while that of Augustus was decorated with ivory and gold (Suetonius, *Julius Caesar*, 84; Toynbee 1971, 58). A wax image of Septimius Severus was burnt in Rome on an ivory couch decorated with gold cloth, as his body had already been cremated at his place of death at York (*ibid.*, 59-60). In the first centuries BC and AD, other rich people were also buried with elaborate ivory-veneered couches but it seems unlikely, from the high level of workmanship involved and the lack of relevant funerary motifs within their decoration, that they were made specifically for funerals. They were also items of furniture that could not have been produced quickly in the necessarily short time between death and burial.

In other cases, bone-decorated beds may have been specially made as funerary beds. A number of third-century cremations at the cemetery by Brougham Fort, Cumbria, contained bone appliqués or inlay considered to be decoration either from couches or biers. It has been suggested this was a fashion perhaps inspired by Septimius Severus' cremation in York (Cool 2004, 464). While these bone appliqués are not as sophisticated as the first century ivory-veneered couches, they still represent a large investment in time and expense if there was anything other than a token amount of decoration on each couch. There were at least 14 different categories of plaques, including strips decorated with parallel grooves, diagonal grooves or dot-and-ring (originally filled with coloured wax), squares, rectangles, triangles, diamonds, spatula-shaped, and ones decorated with simple human and animal heads (Greep 2004, 273-5). The use of black wax is known from Egypt and from Birdoswald in Cumbria, where red and blue were also observed during conservation work (Cool 2004, 439); these dark colours create a bold contrast with the pale colour of the bone itself (*colour plate 8*).

It is unlikely furniture-makers had the space available to keep a complete bone-decorated funerary bed in stock just on the off-chance that some-one rich enough to afford it would die, but the short length of time between death and burial in a period without refrigeration for, and little preservation of, corpses, would mean there was little time to make a special bed from scratch, especially if it was required for the laying in state and not just the funeral itself. It is possible that the necessary elements for a wooden couch were stored in pieces alongside a supply of pre-prepared appliqués as it would then not take long to assemble them as soon as it were required.

The burning of an expensive decorated bed would have been part of the conspicuous consumption frequently considered necessary for funerals. Incense, perfumed oils, and spices were often burnt on the pyres of the rich, alongside the cloths on the couch and the clothes being worn by the corpse, while mourners on occasion also threw clothes and jewellery into the flames (Cool 2004, 441; Toynbee 1971, 58). However, the funerary couch only seems to have been used with cremations. Coffins were used with inhumation burials, but there is no evidence that they were ever expensively decorated with metal or bone appliqués, even though the coffins were just as certainly destroyed by being buried as couches were by being burnt, and would appear to provide equal opportunities for conspicuous consumption. Coffins were on occasion decorated, as ones made from lead often had images cast into the lead sheet, and it may be that some wooden coffins were highly carved and painted instead of being decorated with appliqués, although this does not have the same connotations of wealth.

Furniture in tombs

For the living

Masonry *triclinia* were sometimes incorporated into tomb complexes so that the living could hold meals in commemoration of the dead, held at the tomb so that the deceased could share it. Some *triclinia* were in gardens or walled compounds attached to the tomb, some were immediately outside the entrance, and some were within it (Dunbabin 2003, figs 72-4). They were similar in design to those set up in the grounds of domestic houses, with sloping bases for mattresses, and fixed tables. Meals were either held during the annual Parentalia festival (13-21 February) when offerings were traditionally made at the graves of relatives and friends, or on certain days requested by the dead, such as the anniversary of their birthday. Some tombs at Pompeii incorporated benches so that passers-by might stop to rest and take the time to read the tomb inscriptions and therefore ensure the dead were not forgotten; the fictional Trimalchio was going to have a sundial at his tomb in order that people using it would read his name (Petronius, *Satyricon*, 71).

For the dead

There was no one consistent belief in an after-life in the Roman world. Some thought the spirits of the dead remained in the tomb, so offerings of food, drink and flowers were made there (sometimes via pipes directly onto the remains themselves). During commemorative meals, portions of food and drink were set aside for the dead as if the spirit was above ground with the other diners

(Toynbee 1971, 51). Others believed the spirit moved on, and the corpse was provided with a coin to pay the ferryman in the Underworld, or footwear was added as grave-goods, possibly for use on the journey. The after-life did not apparently require the deceased to bring with them the tools of their trade or any possessions that reflected their status, as the dead are rarely buried with their weapons or tools, and rarely have anything other than a few personal items or food offerings.

Furniture in graves is rare, although all-wood items would generally be difficult to detect. Some cremations were buried in wooden boxes, and some women were buried with a small box containing jewellery, but it was the contents that were of importance, not the container. Iron folding stools have been found in a number of graves, although the significance is unclear. On the one hand their inclusion suggests the seat might be some form of status indicator, while on the other hand artistic evidence suggests that iron stools were common and used by a wide range of people in a variety of every-day occupations.

Tombstones and sarcophagi often show reliefs of the living at work or in other scenes of daily life that included items of furniture, but these scenes were for the benefit of the living. An unusual exception is the Simpelveld sarcophagus from Leiden, where, in an impressive display of workmanship, the sculpted images are on the inside and thus only visible to the body laid in it when the stone sarcophagus was sealed. The deceased, a woman, is shown reclining on a couch, surrounded by different pieces of furniture including a large but visually very plain chest (*colour plates 10* and *11*). There is no suggestion that the arrangement is intended to represent a complete room, since the (empty) dining-table is not placed near the couch, and tucked between the couch and a table/stand is a complete building, usually identified as a bath-house. It is an unusual example of furniture being shown simply as objects and not just incidentally while in use, but the exact reasoning behind this unique sarcophagus must lie in the dead woman's own beliefs in the afterlife and is therefore lost with her.

Some furniture left in tombs was for use by the spirits of the dead. Two stone versions of a wicker chair were found in an underground tomb-chamber at Köln-Weiden (*56*, right). There was room for 29 niches for cremation urns set in the walls round three recesses that have been identified as imitating couches for use by the spirits (Toynbee 1971, 214). The two seats, not intended for use by the living since even the cushions are depicted in stone, may have been for the use of female spirits, leaving the 'couches' for the male spirits, as in life.

17
Conclusion

In the Roman world, as now, the quality and quantity of furniture depended on the owner's wealth and the size of the house to be furnished. It could range from dining-couches and tables made by skilled craftsmen in rare woods and decked out with expensive cloths, to home-made three-legged stools made from whatever wood was at hand. There were antiques and items worth enormous sums of money, that were designed to impress, on display in the houses of the wealthy, and practical furniture falling apart from age in the attic apartments of the poor, sharing nothing in common but their names.

The Romans originally borrowed the design of many items of furniture from the Greeks, but as usual adapted it to suit their own, very different, way of life. The Roman way of formal dining, which appears in theory to be similar to the Greek, was in fact very distinct from it, and the furniture reflected this. In the same way, although many items of furniture appear similar to modern parallels, Roman society was very different to ours and the way they used the rooms in their houses, and therefore the furniture within them, was also very different.

Although there are some regional variations, Roman-style furniture spread quickly throughout the Empire, presumably as a result of the adaptation of Roman architecture and other forms of culture. As a result the same designs of furniture such as tables and couches can be found in every province. In most places, the appearance of the furniture has to be taken from art, since furniture is not a common archaeological site-find. Outside of Herculaneum and Pompeii, few complete items have ever been found as furniture tends to be both big and bulky, and normally made mainly from organic components. Usually only fragments survive, such as detached metal fittings or the occasional piece of waterlogged wood, such as the piece of cupboard from Hayton and the leg from Cramond. Despite this, even these small pieces can reveal new designs not seen in art, and prove there is still much to be learnt about the detail of Roman furniture.

Glossary

Abacus	side-table
Aedicula	shrine
Amphora	large pottery vessel for transporting wine, oil, fish-sauce and other foodstuffs
Arca	box or chest
Archil	type of lichen
Armarium	cupboard
Atrium	a hall with a central shallow pool
Biclinium	two dining-couches set in an L-shape
Bisellium	double seat: a rare type, awarded as a mark of honour
Cartubulum	rectangular table used for holding water containers
Cathedra	high-backed chair
Compluvium	the gape in the roof above the pool in an *atrium*
Culcita	mattress
Fulcrum	wooden pillow or mattress support, often decorated with bronze fittings
Gaunaca	Babylonian fur
Grabatus	simple form of bed
Impluvium	shallow pool in the entrance hall of an *atrium* house
Lectus	general term for bed or couch
Lodix	counterpane or top covering for a bed
Marquetry	use of veneers in different woods or materials to form patterns
Mantelium	table-cloth, napkin and towel
Matta	mat
Mensa	general term for a table
Mortise	a recess designed to hold a projecting tenon to form a secure joint
Nereids	sea nymphs
Oecus	used by modern scholars to describe an open-sided room overlooking a garden or courtyard
Peristromata	decorated bed or couch cover
Prelum	clothes press
Pressorium	clothes press
Pulvinus	pillow (*pulvinar* = couch of pillows for gods)
Rail	horizontal bar at front of a seat
Reno	reindeer skin
Repositorium	tray

Sagum	thick cloak, also used as bed-clothes
Sandapila	cheap bier
Scabellum	foot-stool
Scamnum	stool
Sella	general term for seat
Sella aurea	gold seat: awarded as a sign of honour
Sella curulis	magistrate's seat
Sigma	semi-circular cushion placed on the ground for picnics, also used of semi-circular couches
Solium	seat, including a throne
Stibadium	semi-circular couch
Stragula	a general term for cloth covering or 'throw', including for beds
Stretcher	wooden or metal bar stretching between two other elements, such as bed or table legs, to keep them rigid so that they do not splay out under pressure
Subsellium	bench
Tapete	thick cover, often decorated, used on beds
Teges	mat
Tenon	a projection designed to fit into a mortise to form a secure joint
Tomentum	mattress and pillow/cushion stuffing
Toral	couch cover
Triclinium	word for both dining-room and the set of three couches used in one
Vela	curtain or hanging
Volute	spiral scroll

Bibliography

The translation of Clement of Alexandria comes from that published in *The Ante-Nicene Christian Library*, and that of Augustine's *Against Faustus the Manichean* from *The Nicene and Post-Nicene Fathers*. All other translations taken from Loeb editions, unless otherwise stated. The wording has sometimes been adapted for consistency in the terms used.

Allason-Jones, L. 1989 *Women in Roman Britain*

Allason-Jones, L. and Bishop, M. C. 1988 *Excavations at Roman Corbridge: the Hoard*

Allison, P. M. 2004 *Pompeian Households: an Analysis of the Material Culture*

Bidwell, P. T. and Speak, S. C. 1994 *The Excavations at South Shields Roman Fort, Volume 1*

Birley, A. 2002 *Garrison Life at Vindolanda: a Band of Brothers*

Blanc, N. and Nercessiou, A. 1992 *La Cuisine Romaine Antique*

Blanchard-Lemée, M., Ennaïfer, M., Slim, H. and Slim, L. 1996 *Mosaics of Roman Africa: Floor Mosaics from Tunisia*

Boon, G. C. 1983 Some Romano-British domestic shrines and their inhabitants, in B. Hartley and J. Wacher (eds), *Rome and her Northern Provinces,* 33-55

Bustacchini, G. undated *Ravenna: Capital of Mosaic*

Carroll, M. 2001 *Romans, Celts and Germans: the German Provinces of Rome*

Cantarella, E. 1999 *Pompeji: Liebe und Erotik in einre römischen Stadt*

CIL = *Corpus Inscriptionum Latinarum*

Colledge, M. A. R. 1976 *The Art of Palmyra*

Cool, H. E. M. 2004 *The Roman Cemetery at Brougham, Cumbria, Excavations 1966-7*

Cooley, A. E. and Cooley, M. G. 2004 *Pompeii: a Sourcebook*

Cornell, T. and Matthews, J. 1982 *Atlas of the Roman World*

Crummy, N. 1983 *Colchester Archaeological Report 2: The Roman Small Finds from Excavations in Colchester 1971-9*

Crummy, P. 1984 *Colchester Archaeological Report 3: Excavations at Lion Walk, Balkerne Lane and Middleborough, Colchester, Essex*

Dalby, A. 1998 *Cato: on Farming*

de Franciscis, A. 1978 *The Buried Cities: Pompeii and Herculaneum*

dell'Orto, L. F. and Varone, A. 1992 *Rediscovering Pompeii*

Dietz, K., Osterhaus, U., Rieckhoff-Pauli, S. and Spindler, K. 1979 *Regensburg zur Römerzeit*

Dosi, A. and Schnell, F. 1986 *I Romani in Cucina*

Douet, J. 1998 *British Barracks 1600-1914: their Architecture and Role in Society*

Dunbabin, K. 1991 *Triclinium* and *stibadium*, in Slater 1991, 121-48

Dunbabin, K. 2003 *The Roman Banquet: Images of Conviviality*

Ellis, S. P. 2000 *Roman Housing*

Erim, K. T. and Reynolds, J. 1970 The copy of Diocletian's Edict on maximum prices from Aphrodisias in Caria, *Journal of Roman Studies,* **60**, 120–41

Espérandieu, E. 1965 *Recueil Général des Bas-reliefs Statues et Bustes de la Gaule Romaine,* (reprint)

Felletti Maj, B. 1940 *Civiltà Romana: la Casa e l'Arredamento*

Flanders, J. 2003 *The Victorian House*

George, M. 1997 *Servus* and *domus*: the slave in the Roman house, in R. Laurence and A. Wallace-Hadrill (eds), *Domestic Space in the Roman World: Pompeii and Beyond*

Grabar, A. 1966 *The Beginning of Christian Art, 200-395*

Grant, M. 1979 *The Art and Life of Pompeii and Herculaneum*

Graser, E. R. 1975 The Edict of Diocletian, in T. Frank, *An Economic Survey of Ancient Rome, Volume 5: Rome and Italy of the Empire,* 305–421

Greep, S. 2004 Bone and antler veneer, in Cool 2004

Hartley, E., Hawkes, J., Henig, M. and Mee, F. 2006 *Constantine the Great: York's Roman Emperor*

Haug, F. 1919 Römische Kellertische, *Germania,* **3**, 102–9

Holmes, N. and Raisen, P. 2000 Objects of wood, in N. Holmes, *Excavation of Roman Sites at Cramond, Edinburgh,* Edinburgh

Horn, H. G. 1987 *Die Römer in Nordrhein-Westfalen*

Huskinson, J. 1996 *Roman Children's Sarcophagi: their Decoration and Social Significance*

Jackson, R. 1988 *Doctors and Diseases in the Roman Empire*

Jashemski, W. F. 1979 *The Gardens of Pompeii, Herculaneum and the Villas Destroyed by Vesuvius*

Jashemski, W. F. 1987 Recently excavated gardens and cultivated land of the villas at Boscoreale and Oplontis, in E. B. MacDougall (ed.), *Ancient Roman Villa Gardens*

Jessup, R. 1954 Excavation of a Roman barrow at Holdborough, Snodland, *Archaeologia Cantiana,* **67**, 1–61

Johns, C. 1982 *Sex or Symbol: Erotic Images of Greece and Rome*

Kleiner, D. 1992 *Roman Sculpture*

Kocsis, L. and Tóth, E. 2005 The Roman Age, in *Guide to the Archaeological Exhibition of the Hungarian National Museum 400,000 BC to 804 AD*

Kraus, T. 1975 *Pompeii and Herculaneum*

Lawson, A. J. 1976 Shale and jet objects from Silchester, *Archaeologia,* **105**, 241–75

Liversidge, J. 1955 *Furniture in Roman Britain*

MacDonald, G. and Curle, A. O. 1929 *The Roman Wall in Scotland*

Mols, S. T. A. M. 1999 *Wooden Furniture in Herculaneum: Form, Technique and Function*

Nichols, R. V. 1979 A Roman couch in Cambridge, *Archaeologia,* **106**, 1–32

O'Leary, T. J. 1989 *Pentre Farm, Flint 1976-81. An Official Building in the Roman Lead Mining District*

Pfister, R. and Bellinger, L. 1945 *The Excavations at Dura-Europos Final Report IV, Part II: The Textiles*

Phillips Barker, E. 1932 *Seneca's Letters to Lucilius*

Pirozzi, M. 2003 *Herculaneum: the Excavations, Local History and Surroundings*

Richter, G. M. A. 1966 *The Furniture of the Greeks, Etruscans and Romans*

Rieche, A. 1984 *Römische Kinder und Gesellschaftsspiele*

Rossiter, J. 1991 *Convivium* and the villa in late antiquity, in Slater 1991, 199–214

Salzman, M. R. 1990 *On Roman Time: the Codex-Calendar of 354 and the Rhythms of Urban Life in Late Antiquity*

Shelton, K. J. 1981 *The Esquiline Treasure*

Slater, W. 1991 *Dining in a Classical Context*

Solley. T. W. 1979 Romano-British side-tables and chip-carving, *Britannia,* **10**, 169–177

Spinazzola, V. 1953 *Pompei, Alla Luce degli Scavi Nuovi di Via dell'Abbondanza, 1910-1923*

St Clair, A. 2003 *Carving as Craft. Palatine East and the Greco-Roman Bone and Ivory Carving Tradition*

Stefani, G. (ed.) 2005 *Cibi e Sapori a Pompei e Dintorini*

Steffanelli, L. (ed.) 1990 *Il Bronzo dei Romani Arredo e Suppellettile*

Temkin, O. 1956 *Soranus' Gynecology*

Toynbee, J. M. C. 1971 *Death and Burial in the Roman World*

Trilling, J. 1982 *The Roman Heritage: Textiles from Egypt and the Eastern Mediterranean 300 to 600 AD,* (also published as *Textile Museum Journal* **21**)

Veyne, P. (ed.) 1987 *A History of Private Life, Volume I*

Wanscher, O. 1980 Sella Curulis: *the Folding Stool, an Ancient Symbol of Dignity*

Walker, S. and Bierbrier, M. 1997 *Ancient Faces: Mummy Portraits from Roman Eygpt*

Wallace-Hadrill, A. 1991 Houses and households: sampling Pompeii and Herculaneum, in B. Rawson (ed.), *Marriage, Divorce and Children in Ancient Rome,* 191–227

Ward-Perkins, J. and Claridge, A. 1976 *Pompeii AD79*

Watson, A. 1985 *The Digest of Justinian, Volume 3*

Webster, J. 1989 Objects of stone, in T. J. O'Leary, *Excavations at Pentre Farm, Flint, 1976-81*

Weitzmann, K. 1977 *Late Antique and Early Christian Book Illumination*

Weitzmann, K. 1979 *Age of Spirituality*

Wild, J. P. 1984 The textiles, in Crummy 1984, 44-7

Index

shrines 132, 133, **134**
stools 98, **99**, 106, **plate 6**
tables 69, 70, **85**, 86, 159
Suburban Baths 112
Villa of the Papyri 131
Hildesheim (Germany) 24, 79
Hinges 24, **126**–7, 138
Holborough (Kent) 102, **103**, 104
Houses and buildings
apartments 156
cottages 150–1
farms 151–4
multiple-room houses 155–67
public buildings 172–7
rich people 168–71

Igel Monument (Germany) 80, 89, **90**, **91**, 120
Imperial furniture 170–1, 180
Inlay 28–30, 127
Inns 173–**4**
Iron 23, 102–4
Ivory **26**, 27, 28–9, 37–8

Kitchens 89–**91**, 130, 137, **163**–5
Köln-Weiden (Germany) **118**, 119, 182

Law courts 175–6
Libraries 161
Living-rooms 162

Maple wood 21, **plates 3–4, 6**
Marbella (Spain) 137, **163**–4
Marble 23, 112, **113**
Masonry
beds and couches 43-**44**, **53**–4, **plate 12**
benches 112–14
shelves **135**, 137
shrines 132–3, **134**
tables **53**, 77
Mats 149
Mattresses 56–8
covers **50**, 63, 64, 66–**7**, **plate 16**
Metal
decoration 29–30, 35–7
stools and benches 102–4, 110–12, **plate 17**
tables **71**, 88
types used 23–4
Military furniture 177–8
Mosaic
floors 48, **49**, 149
wood **25**–6, **plate 6**
Moth deterrents 127, 140–1
Mumrills (Antonine Wall) 112, **113**

Neumagen (Germany) 89, **90**
Nijmegen (Netherlands) **100**, 101

North-west provinces
chairs **90**, **119**–20
tables 69–70, 72, 74
see also specific countries and sites

Oak 22
Olive wood 22
Ostia
cupboards **125**, 130, **plate 16**
inns 173,**174**
mattress 66, **plate 16**
stools and footstools 104, 110, **plate 16**
tables 87, 91, **93**, **94**

Packing cases 141
Paint 30
Palmyra (Syria) 51, 66, **67**
Pearl decoration 30
Pentre Farm (Flint) 112, **113**
Peristyles 156, 157–8
Piazza Armerina (Sicily) **142**, 143
Pillow-rests 29, 33, 34, 35–7
Pillows 56–8, 63
Polgárdi (Hungary) 24
Polishes 30–1
Pompeii
beds and couches 52, **53**, 49
benches 110–12, **plate 17**
boxes and chests **139**, 140, 141
brothels 40, 43
cupboards 127, **128**, 129, 131,132, 157
decorative features 28, 30
felt-maker's shop 115, 174–**5**
Forum Baths 110, **111**
Gladiator Training School 30
House *VI,17,41* 131
House of Cornelius Rufus 85
House of Iulius Polybius 127, 156
House of M. Lucretius Fronto **87**
House of Menander 79, 140
House of the Red Walls 133
House of the Blacksmith 124, **125**
House of the Chaste Lovers 66
House of the *Cryptoporticus* **53**, 127
House of the *Ephebus* 28
House of the Theatrical Pictures 157
House of the Tragic Poet **134**
House of the Trojan Shrine 28, 127
House of the Vettii **128**, 129, 132
inns and taverns 112, 173, **plates 17–18**
shrines 132, 133, **134**
Small Theatre 176
stool 100
tables **71**, 79, 83, 85, **86**, **87**, **88**, 92
Tavern *VI,14,36* 173
textiles 66